A. M. HUNTER

EXPLORING
the
NEW TESTAMENT

THE SAINT ANDREW PRESS
EDINBURGH

© A. M. HUNTER 1971

First published in 1971
by the Saint Andrew Press
121 *George Street, Edinburgh*

ISBN 07152 0159 X

The poem on page 119 by G. A. Studdert-Kennedy
"He Was a Gambler Too", from *The Unutterable
Beauty,* is printed by permission of Messrs Hodder
& Stoughton Ltd.

Printed in Great Britain by
Neill & Co. Ltd., Edinburgh

EXPLORING THE NEW TESTAMENT

A WORD ABOUT THE WORDS

Here (to adapt a phrase of Ivor Brown's) is 'a New Testament Word in your ear' or, rather, sixty-four of them. The first reaction may well be, 'Not another one surely! Haven't we already Professor Barclay's word-studies, Alan Richardson's *Theological Word Book of the Bible,* above all, the monumental *Theological Dictionary of the New Testament,* a German master-piece, begun in 1933 under Kittel's editorship, which G. W. Bromiley, with incredible industry, is now translating into lucid English?'

My defence must be that this is one with a difference. It is not systematic or exhaustive, but personal, idiosyncratic, discursive. Many of my word-studies are in the nature of brief essays where the personal equation or the 'modern application' is more permissible than in the conventional dictionary discussion. So I have wandered through the New Testament from the Sermon on the Mount in Matthew to the Seer's vision of the Holy City in Revelation, picking out words which modern scholars have illumined with fresh meaning. Moreover, I have interpreted 'Word' in the broadest sense. Sometimes it is a single word like 'mansion' or 'charisma'; sometimes a phrase like 'ransom for many' or 'a thorn in the flesh'; and occasionally a chapter (like Acts 27) or even a whole book (like 'Jude the obscure').

My selection includes business nouns (like *koinōnia*) banking verbs like *apechō* ('paid in full'), a legal term like 'advocate' (paraclete) or a medical one like 'paregoric'. Always I have tried to keep in mind the truth of Ritschl's dictum, 'The Old Testament is the lexicon of the New', of which 'gospel' is a good example. So you will find here not only the odd Hebrew or Aramaic word (*e.g.* Amen and *Abba*) but Greek words stained with Hebrew meanings like *doxa* ('glory'), as you will also find Greek words like *agapē* ('love')

5

or *charis* ('grace') which the Gospel baptized with new meaning.

I have made liberal use of modern translations, chiefly the New English Bible and the Revised Standard Version, but also the Jerusalem Bible and the versions of Moffatt and Knox. Moreover, before I closed a causerie on a 'Word', I have tried to give it a modern application, without I trust, becoming tiresomely 'edifying' (though the New Testament is, in the best sense of the word, 'an edifying book'). If there are Scotticisms in my book like 'thrawn', this is not only because I believe that the Scots sometimes have the *mot juste* for a word in the Greek New Testament, but also because I cannot—and would not—forget 'the hole of the pit whence I was digged'.

CONTENTS

1. 'Amen I tell you'

(*Matthew 6.2 etc.*)

Of all the slang we have borrowed from the United States, OK (or Okay) is that in widest currency. Whether it was originally the Choctaw *oke* ('So be it' or 'It is so') or, perhaps more probably, a humorous abbreviation of 'All correct', is a matter of debate. What is certain is that it has become with us an almost universal formula of confirmation—a kind of secular Amen.

Now, if somebody in our hearing were to *preface* his statements with an 'Okay I tell you', this would certainly strike us as odd, and we might resent the suggestion of self-claimed authority which it carried. Jesus did just this with what we might call the most famous of all words of assent—Amen. He said, 'Amen I tell you'—and nobody else, so far as we know, ever did.

As every student of the Bible is aware, 'Amen' is a Hebrew word meaning 'truly' which the Jews used at the end of a prayer, doxology, sermon, or scripture reading, to endorse the words of their spokesman. It was the congregation's corroborative 'Yes'—a kind of holy 'Hear! Hear!'—binding them to what had just been said. 'Amen', said one of their rabbis, 'is confirmation, Amen is protestation, Amen is assent.' And by their Amens the Jews set great store. 'If a man lengthens his Amen,' said another rabbi, 'God will lengthen his life.' This sonorous 'So let it be' the early Church took over, as the New Testament shows (e.g. Rom. 16.27, 1 Cor. 14.16, 1 Peter 4.11) and they used it very much as Old Israel had done.

Our interest, now, however, is not the early Christian's use of Amen but Christ's. He did not use it as they did at, say, the end of a doxology or thanksgiving. When he had some-

9

thing momentous to say, he *prefaced* it with an Amen: 'Amen I tell you.' And you may search Jewish literature from end to end for a precise parallel to this.

The formula in fact bears on the whole question of Jesus' authority. When a modern policeman says, 'in the name of the Law' he invokes earthly authority; and there can be little doubt that when Jesus said, 'Amen I tell you', he spoke with some kind of divine authority. For analogy we naturally think of the Old Testament prophet's 'Thus saith the Lord'. But no prophet ever dared to say, 'Amen I tell you.' Clearly when Jesus utters his unique Amen, he is not simply guaranteeing on his own authority that what follows is true and trustworthy. Rather is he implying that his proclamation is not his own but God's, that he only passes on what he has himself received—from on high.

Altogether the formula occurs seventy-four times in the Gospels and is limited to the sayings of Jesus. Luke yields the fewest examples—only six: Matthew with thirty, the most; and one curious feature of John's twenty-five examples is that he doubles the Amen: 'Amen, Amen I tell you'.

What kind of statements does this Amen of Jesus preface? Study the 13 examples of it in the earliest Gospel, Mark, and you find that about two-thirds of them have to do with the Kingdom of God which he proclaimed—indeed embodied—or his own person and destiny. And it is much the same in the other Gospels, though Luke has a tendency to replace the Hebrew word 'Amen' with the Greek for 'truly'.

Some of Jesus' Amen sayings, to be sure, are more general. 'Amen I tell you' introduces, for example, his praise of the Gentile centurion's faith (Matt. 8.10), his ironical words about the 'reward' of the hypocrites (Matt. 6.2, 6, 16), his sayings about mountain-moving faith (Mark 11.23) or the widow's mite (Mark 12.43). But, for the most part, the Amen statements deal, directly or indirectly, with the Kingdom of God and the part he himself plays in its coming.

On the one hand, this Amen prefaces his words about the blessedness of the disciples who are now seeing what prophets and righteous men had longed in vain to see—the Kingdom (Matt. 13.17); his declaration that, if men are to enter it,

10

they must receive it as a child receives a present from his parent's hand (Mark 10.15); his assertion that the least in the Kingdom is greater than John the Baptist (Matt. 11.11); his prediction that at no distant time the Kingdom will have come 'with power' (Mark 9.1); his self-denying word at the Last Supper, 'I shall not drink again of the fruit of the vine until that day when I drink it new in the Kingdom of God' (Mark 14.25).

On the other hand, Amen introduces sayings about Jesus' own person, mission and destiny. A doubled Amen compares his own relation with God to that between an apprenticed son and his father (John 5.19f). An Amen saying promises blessings and reward to all who have sacrificed home-ties for his sake (Mark 10.29). 'Amen, Amen I tell you' prefaces the saying about the grain of wheat in which Jesus speaks of his suffering and death and the rich harvest it will bring (John 12.24); and in the great picture of the Last Judgment (Matt. 25.31-46), 'Amen I tell you' introduces his 'as you did it to one of the least of these my brethren, you did it to me'. A like Amen prefaces his promise on the Cross to the penitent thief (Luke 23.43).

Quite clearly 'Amen I tell you' is what the learned men call an *ipsissima vox* of Jesus, an authentic feature of his way of speaking. We may fairly surmise that it had its origin in his own awareness of being the bearer of God's Kingdom to men and in his own unique experience of Abba Father who was the King in that Kingdom. It suggests the certainty of one who knows and promulgates because he has himself first learned from his heavenly Father. Always it connotes his authority and gives validity to what he says. 'He makes good the word, not the word him.' So Schlier, who writes the article about it in Kittel's *Theological Dictionary of the New Testament*,[1] can say: 'In the "Amen" preceding the "I tell you" of Jesus we have the whole of Christology in a nutshell.' If this perhaps sounds like an exaggeration, Jesus' use of Amen must always be included in the evidence to be reckoned with when we seek to answer the question, 'What think ye of Christ? Whose son is he?' The answer is, 'He is the One

[1] Vol. I, 338.

who speaks as his Father has bidden him' (John 12.49), and therefore speaks with divine authority.

2. The Humanity of God

(Matthew 6.11)

'Theology has had many talents in our time' wrote Alasdair McIntyre, 'but no other genius.' He was referring to the great Swiss theologian, Karl Barth who died in 1968. One of the marks of Barth's greatness is that late in life he was not ashamed to admit the need of a better answer to the question who and what God is than the one he had given when he began his career. Away back in the 'twenties' when his continual complaint was that men had lost the sense of the majesty and mystery of God and made him all 'too human', he spoke of God as 'wholly other', as a Being veiled and mysterious, not to be discovered anywhere in this world or to be described by human analogies. But twelve years before his death, confessing that the exigencies of the time had made him go too far, he made the *amende honorable* in a book entitled *The Humanity of God*. (Since then an American admirer has compiled an excellent book about him called *How I Changed My Mind*.[1])

For, of course, Jesus, in whom Barth said man had all he needs to know about God, did not regard God as 'wholly other'. On the contrary he believed earthly and human analogies could figure forth to men God's nature and will. For Jesus, human experience was a kind of spring-board for the adventure of faith. He had a way of saying to his disciples, 'Take the very best you know: God is all that—and far more.' So, taking the highest values in human life, he invited his disciples to project them into the unseen world and find in them a reflection of him whom he called Lord of heaven and earth.

[1] The Saint Andrew Press.

12

'If . . . how much more' (Gk. *posō mallon*) was Jesus' argument, and it is in his 'how much more's (what the logician would call his *a fortiori* arguments) that we find the evidence for the humanity of God. Once, in the Sermon on the Mount, his 'how much more' appeals not to human but to wild nature, 'If God so clothes the grass of the field which today is, and tomorrow is cast into the oven, how much more will he clothe you, you little-faiths' (Matt. 6.30). But normally it is to human nature that he appeals, as in the Parable of the Asking Son (Matt. 7.9-11; Luke 11.11-13):

'What man among you, if his son asks him for a loaf, will give him a stone?

Or if he asks for a fish, will give him a snake?

Of if he asks for an egg, will give him a scorpion?

If you then, bad as you are, know how to give your children what is good for them, how much more will your heavenly Father give good things to those who ask him.'

And even in parables where there is no 'how much more', the same kind of argument is implied. Take the parable of The Friend at Midnight (Luke 11.5-8), which would be better called 'The Grumpy Neighbour'. 'If even a man with so many reasons for being disobliging,' says Jesus in effect, 'can be moved to give you what you ask, how much more will God lend a ready ear to his children's requests!'

Nor is it otherwise in the story of The Importunate Widow (Luke 18.2-8) which ought to be renamed 'The Callous Judge', since he is the chief character in it. Jesus is not here describing some dourly ungracious Deity who needs to be badgered into compliance. As in 'The Grumpy Neighbour', the argument is 'by contraries'. If even this unprincipled judge could be moved by the widow's importunity, how much more will God answer his people's prayers for vindication!

Thus, by his 'how much more's' from human experience, Jesus lifts his hearers to higher levels of trust and conviction, forces on them the simple certainties about God, declares the humanity of the Almighty.

We come back to Barth with whom we began. It was one of Barth's great sayings that 'God has said Yes to men in

13

Jesus Christ'. But if this is so, Christ's human analogies in the Gospels are part of that 'Yes', and a not unimportant part. By all means let us agree that the whole majesty and mystery of God cannot be enclosed in the obvious appearances of the world; but, with Jesus' teaching before us, let not any talk about God's 'wholly-otherness' shroud in grim denial the bright encouragement of the parables.

3. The Face of Christ

(*Matthew 17.2*)

Dennis Potter's television play *The Son of Man* raised afresh questions which have exercised the Christian imagination down nineteen centuries. What did Christ look like? Was he tall or short? What kind of features had he? What hue was his hair? What colour were his eyes?

It cannot be said that the Gospels are forthcoming with the answers. Your modern biographer will tell you what his hero looked like, in youth, at the prime of his life, in old age; and a writer of genius like Carlyle will, in a few vivid sentences, limn to the life a Charles Lamb or a Lord Tennyson. But the evangelists were not biographers, or even 'Boswellisers', of Jesus. To be sure, Luke had a gift for miniature pen-portraits, but, though better than any other he shows us 'the kneeling Christ', he has not depicted his features for us. The truth is that the Gospel writers were not concerned to describe for posterity the lineaments of the Son of Man. They tell us something of his emotions—that he could look on a man with love (Mark 10.21) and round on another with rebuke (Mark 8.33), that he could be moved with great compassion for a crowd (Mark 6.34) and that he could 'fume inwardly' at Lazarus's grave (John 11.33), that he could 'exult' (Luke 10.21) and that he could 'weep' (John 11.35. Luke 19.41). But of his face they have little to say save that on the Mount of Transfiguration it 'shone like the sun' (Matt. 17.2) and that

14

he 'hardened his face' as he began his march on Jerusalem (Luke 9.51). The rest of the New Testament has little to add. In Rev. 1.12-16 the Seer tells us that the eyes of the glorified Christ 'flamed like fire', that his hair was 'as snow-white wool', and that his voice was 'like the sound of rushing waters'. But, as the passage is a tissue of Old Testament phrases designed to suggest the splendour and authority of Christ in glory, we can hardly use it to paint a portrait of the earthly Son of Man.

Yet, human nature being what it is, men were bound later to supply from their imaginations what the evangelists did not tell; and in early Christian literature we find two quite different conceptions of the face of Christ. The writer of the apocryphal Acts of Thomas and others pictured an *ugly* Christ. Strange as it may seem to us, this liking for an uncomely Christ is not hard to account for. Was it not written in that famous prophecy of Isaiah which Christians believed was fulfilled in Christ:

'Without beauty, without majesty we saw him:
No looks to attract our eyes' (Isa. 53.3 Jer. Bible)?

Yet with such a picture most Christians could not rest content. Jesus was 'the good (*kalos*) shepherd' and did not *kalos* describe what was outwardly beautiful? (In John 10.11,14 *kalos* means not 'beautiful' but 'true'—describes one who really has the right to call himself a shepherd, because he is prepared to die for his sheep). Had it not been said in Ps. 45, which they applied to Christ, 'You are the fairest of the sons of men'? Study the earliest picture of Christ in the catacomb of St. Priscilla, and it is a *handsome,* not an ugly, Christ that meets your eyes through the dust and grime of eighteen centuries. Youth and beauty belong to the statuette of the Good Shepherd, now in the Lateran Museum, which once adorned a third-century Roman crypt.

How some Christians of the Middle Ages pictured Christ we may learn from the Letter of Lentulus. Purporting to be a letter to the Roman senate from a Roman official in Judea in the reign of the Emperor Tiberius, it describes Jesus as middling tall and straight in body, with hair parted in the middle and the colour of an unripe hazel nut; curled locks

15

falling below his ears and a forked beard; a smooth brow, a faultless nose, an unwrinkled face, with eyes grey and clear.

The Letter is not a contemporary pen-portrait by a Roman who saw Jesus in Palestine; on the contrary it dates from the thirteenth century and was probably composed in Italy. But it shows how medieval piety conceived of the earthly Christ. And so down succeeding centuries they went on picturing him. 'Fairest Lord Jesus' is how one of the best-beloved hymns of the 17th century addressed him.

Yet beauty is not necessarily truth; and, as we move into modern times, with the stress, especially in the nineteenth century, falling more and more on the theme, 'Jesus, divinest when thou most art man', we find the handsome Christ yielding place to an *ordinary* Christ, a Christ with 'no form or comeliness' to distinguish him from other men. Turgenev has told how once, as he worshipped in a simple country church, suddenly a man was by his side who, he felt, must be Christ. But—he had 'a face like all men's faces'. 'What sort of Christ is this?' he mused. 'Such an ordinary, ordinary man.' At last however the truth came home to him: 'I realised that just such a face—a face like all men's faces—is the face of Christ.'

There is truth of course in this: 'He had to be made like his brethren in every respect' (Heb. 2.17) must mean, among other things, that he had a human face: so Browning saw:

> O Saul,
> It shall be a Face like my face that receives thee.

And yet, if the human face is at all a mirror of the soul within—as, for Wordsworth, Newton's 'prism and silent face' was the index of his mighty mind—the Son of Man's can have been no ordinary face.

However little the Gospels tell us of Christ's features, they suggest on every page something of the spirit that dwelt within. P. T. Forsyth[1] has put it into words:

'Lord of himself and all besides; with an irresistible power to force, and even hurry, events on a world scale; and yet with the soul that sat among children, and the heart in which

[1] *The Person and Place of Jesus Christ*, 65f.

16

children sat. He had an intense reverence for the past that yet
was too small for him. It rent him to rend it, and yet he had
to break it up, to the breaking of his own heart, in the greatest
revolution the world ever saw. He was an austere man, a
severe critic, a born fighter, of choleric wrath and fiery scorn
so that people thought he was Elijah or John the Baptist; yet
he was gentle in the last degree, especially with those ignorant
and out of the way. In the thick of life he yet stood detached,
sympathetic yet aloof, cleaving at once both to men and to
solitude. With a royal, and almost proud, sense of himself,
he poured out his soul to God, and to death, and was the
friend of publicans and sinners.'

If these words at all justly paint his spiritual lineaments,
who will say that Christ's must have been just 'a face like all
men's faces'? And if, by the mercy of God, you and I one day
see Christ in his glory, will not the face that welcomes us be
one in which his majesty is conjoined with meekness and
strength is made perfect in love?[1]

4. Thrawn Generation

(Matthew 17.17)

'The Greeks,' the saying goes, 'had a word for it.' But so,
on occasion, have the Scots—for the Greek.

'O faithless and perverse generation,' says Jesus at the foot
of the Mount of Transfiguration, sadly marvelling at his
contemporaries' unbelief and absorbed in the thought of his
approaching death, 'how long am I to be with you, how long
am I to put up with you?' 'Perverse' translates the Greek
diestrammene, which is the perfect participle passive of
diastrepho 'twist'. 'Thrawn', the past participle of 'thraw'

---

[1] My friend Dr. William Lillie suggests that the artists who pictured
a handsome Christ were doing what William Blake claimed to do—
limning the inner essence, not the outward appearance.

which is the English 'throw' with the old sense of 'twist' preserved in it, is the perfect equivalent of the Greek.

Sometimes the word retains its literal meaning. One thinks of Robert Louis Stevenson's famous short story about poor Janet with the twisted neck—'thrawn Janet'. More commonly it bears its figurative meaning—twisted in one's 'inner heart', not only 'dour' (sullenly obstinate) but positively misguided and wrong-headed.

The whole tragedy of old Israel is in that word. 'If I had not come and spoken to them,' said Jesus in the Upper Room, 'if I had not done among them the works which no one else did, they would not be guilty of sin' (John 15.22ff). Pure and unique goodness—God's goodness—had been in action among them, but they had 'thrawnly' refused to recognise it. It is not true that 'we needs must love the highest when we see it'.

5. Gnats and Camels

(Matthew 23.24)

'Ye blind guides which strain at a gnat and swallow a camel.' (AV).

'Blind guides! straining out a gnat and swallowing a camel!' (RSV).

This verse is part of the fifth of eight 'Woes' pronounced by Jesus on the scribes and Pharisees in Matt. 23. On the strength of this and similar passages some have accused Jesus of *cursing* them. This is not true. A curse is a wish, sometimes accompanied by a gesture (like Jennet Clouston's in Stevenson's *Kidnapped*) that evil may befall the person cursed. In fact, our Lord's 'Woes' are not wishes of that kind at all; they are highly emotional statements of fact; and it would be better, as the NEB does, to translate, 'Alas for you, doctors of the law and Pharisees!'

This slur on Christ removed, let us note how the RSV here

18

makes sense of the AV. How the famous forty-seven who made the AV came to write 'at' for 'out' is a mystery. The *Oxford English Dictionary* will not have it that they slipped up—'strain at' is archaic usage for 'strain out'—but it is widely held that the 'at' is a misprint. In any case, the Greek verb *diulizō* undoubtedly means 'I strain out', and this correction at once enables us to see our Lord's vivid picture.

Here is a fastidious Pharisee resolved that nothing unclean shall pass his lips and defile him. He starts to filter what he is going to drink. Over the cup he holds a piece of muslin, and pours with care. Suddenly he stops: he sees a gnat (or 'midge', as the NEB has it) which he quickly flicks away. Now praise be, he is safe from swallowing it. And just then, says Jesus, he swallowed a camel!

'How many of us', comments T. R. Glover,[1] 'have ever pictured the process and the series of sensations as the long hairy neck slid down the throat of the Pharisee—all that amplitude of loose-hung anatomy—the hump—two humps— both of them slid down—and he never noticed—and four legs, all of them—with whole outfit of knees and big padded feet. The Pharisee swallowed a camel—and never noticed it!'

Is there not humour there—hyperbolical humour employed to caricature those who concentrate on trifles to the neglect of the things that really matter? The Pharisees husbanded their rushlights and forgot that there were stars in the sky. Professing to have 'a sense of what is vital in religion' (Rom. 2.18) they got their priorities all wrong, mistaking the minutiae for the magnitudes.

It is very easy for us now to pillory the Pharisees and the scribes; but are there to be no 'Alases' from 'the King and Head of the Church' for those Christians who do the same thing today—no 'Alases' for churchmen who get worked up about details of ritual or liturgy while the wounds in Christ's Body remain unhealed, or millions starve to death for lack of 'Christian Aid', or our teenagers drift into paganism because we will not truly reveal the glory and grandeur of the Gospel?

[1] *The Jesus of History*, 49.

6. The Shekinah Promise

(Matthew 28.20)

However much men may entertain the idea of the omnipresence of God, all worship demands a *praesens numen*—a present deity. Now the Jews believed that the divine presence was specially 'located' in the wilderness tabernacle and, later, in the temple; and the word they used for the local presence of God with his people was the *Shekinah* (from the Hebrew word meaning 'dwelling'). What the risen Christ offers in Matt. 28.20 is a Shekinah promise—his presence with his people to the end of time: 'Lo, I am with you alway, even unto the end of the world.'

Has that promise been kept?

'I will not leave you orphans' had been Jesus' promise to his disciples in the Upper Room (John 14.18). It is the verdict of uncounted Christians down nineteen centuries that he has not gone back on it. From Paul of Tarsus to Sadhu Sundar Singh, from Polycarp of Smyrna to Grenfell of Labrador, from John of Patmos to John White of Glasgow, however their words may differ, the testimony has been the same: 'Christ is alive, and he has had dealings with us, and we with him.'

'No apostle', wrote James Denney[1] in a famous paradox, 'ever remembered Christ'. They had no need to. He was still with them. By his power they healed and blessed. In their trials and tribulations he stood by them. He was with them when they broke the bread. From his unseen throne with the Father he was reigning and guiding the history and the hearts of men to the Kingdom of God, that Kingdom which he was, and is.

Read the inscriptions in the catacombs of Rome, study the hymns of the mediaeval men of God, recall the ringing words of the Reformers, and what are they but one prolonged witness

[1] *Studies in Theology*, 154.

to a living and enabling Christ who still abides, through the Holy Spirit, with his people?

Nor does the chain of witness end with them; it goes on down succeeding centuries.

Samuel Rutherford lies in his Aberdeen jail, and this is what he sets down in his diary: 'Jesus Christ came to me in my cell last night, and every stone glowed like a ruby'.

David Livingstone, journeying through darkest Africa, repeats to himself Christ's Shekinah promise. 'This is the word of a gentleman,' he says.

R. W. Dale paces his study on Easter eve when the reality of the living Christ 'comes on him like a burst of sudden glory'. 'Christ is alive! Christ is alive!' he says, and ever after, the Resurrection becomes the prime article in his creed.

C. F. Andrews testifies to the Christ who has been his constant comrade on 'the Indian Road'. 'I do not picture Jesus as I see him in the Gospel story,' he writes, 'for I have known the secret of his presence, here and now, as a daily reality.'

John White, near the end of his life, describes his early search for faith and in majestic monosyllables tells how he found it: 'I met a Man'.

'My friend in Stoke was ill,' says Charles Raven of the turning-point in his life, 'and I visited him. He was not alone. Jesus was alive and present with my friend, as he had been alive and present with the eleven in the Upper Room. He was alive and present with me.'

But these six witnesses are not alone. Beside them stand millions and millions unknown to fame or the history books, who have borne witness to the perennial presence and power of Christ.

Impressive evidence? Yes, and one might suppose that such a centuries-long argument from experience would come with convincing power to all who heard it. Nevertheless we know that it does not always do so. There are always those who demur and say, 'Think it possible that you—and all like Christians before you—are the victims of one long and colossal delusion. How can you claim objective truth for this experience of Christ, abundantly authenticated though it seems to be? How, for example, does your awareness of Christ as a living Lord differ in essence from that of the simple Catholic lass who claims to be in touch with the saints or the Blessed Virgin Mary?'

To all such objectors the Christian answer is two-fold—first, personal and then, historical. (I here summarise the argument in P. T. Forsyth's greatest book *The Person and Place of Jesus Christ*.[1])

To begin with, we may say, 'If I am not to doubt absolutely everything, I must find practical certainty in what founds and sustains my moral life—especially my new moral life. This for me is Christ. What nature is to the scientist, that Christ is to the believer. Now what I have in Christ is not an evanescent impression but a life changed and renewed. In my inmost experience, tested through the years, he brings me to God—is Immanuel to me. Doubt the validity of my experience if you must, but you must doubt it on the ground of something deeper and surer than the certitude my experience brings me. And there is none—no natural certitude which has a right to challenge the moral one—the moral certitude of my being re-oriented and renewed by Christ.'

Second: to the suggestion that there is no difference between experience of Christ and experience of a saint, there is this historical answer. It is the merest truth that Christ has invaded our human history with a piercing, crucial, moral effect unparalleled by any saint. Indeed, he has entered the life of the whole Church not less than that of the individual. I know Christ, and the Church knows him, as a person uniquely able to create fresh experience of himself, which is experience of God—an experience behind which stands the whole witness of the evangelical succession down the Christian centuries.

It is this two-fold testimony, personal and historical, to the presence and power of Christ as living Saviour which must be the Christian's final answer to all sceptics and doubters. And it is all summed up in T. R. Glover's well-known words: 'The Gospels are not four, but ten thousand times ten thousand, and thousands of thousands, and the last word of every one of them is, "Lo, I am with you alway, even unto the end of the world" '.[2]

[1] Chapter 7.   [2] *The Conflict of Religions*, 140.

22

7. The Gospel of Jesus

(Mark 1.14f)

'The New Testament lies hidden in the Old Testament,' said St. Augustine, 'the Old Testament is made plain in the New.' And if there is one truth the scholars of our time have been re-discovering, it is the paramount importance of the Old Testament as a key to the New. There is no better example of this than the word 'gospel'.

Every student knows that 'gospel'—a fine old English word from *god spel* 'good news'—exactly translates the Greek compound word *euangelion* 'good news'. (The verb to 'announce good news' is *euangelizesthai*). But not every student knows that the 'good news' Jesus announced—and indeed embodied—really goes back to the 'good news' preached by the man we call 'Isaiah of Babylon' whose prophecies begin with the famous words 'Comfort ye, comfort ye, my people, saith your God'. (Isa. 40.1.)

How can this be?

Behind our two New Testament Greek words lies the Hebrew root *bsr*. This gives us the noun *besōrah* and the verb *bissar* which are Hebrew for 'good news' and the telling of it. In the earlier books of the Old Testament[1] they are used in a secular sense, often of the 'good news' of victory in battle. But in the prophecies of Isa. 40-66 the Hebrew words acquire a theological—indeed we may say, a messianic—meaning. These passages furnish the key to the word 'gospel' as Jesus used it.

Let us start by recalling that, when Jesus preached in the synagogue at Nazareth, he read from Isa. 61:

'The Spirit of the Lord is upon me,

Because he has anointed me to preach good tidings to the poor . . .' and, as he sat down, declared, 'Today this scripture

[1] See, for example, 2 Sam. 4.10 and 18.22.

23

has been fulfilled in your hearing' (Luke 4.16-21). This is the clue to our Lord's use of the word 'gospel'.

More than half a millenium before what Paul calls 'the fulness of time' (Gal. 4.4) Isaiah had prophesied the return of the exiles. He foresaw them coming back triumphantly to Jerusalem with God in their midst and a herald going before them with a proclamation of 'good news'. Thrice (Isa. 40.9, 41.27 and 52.7) there is the promise of 'one who brings good news'; but it is in the last passage that we see most clearly the link between the Old and New Testaments, between Isaiah and Jesus. All Jerusalem is pictured on the walls when suddenly on the hill-top there appears the herald with good tidings:

> How beautiful upon the mountains
> are the feet of the herald,
> Who brings good news of peace,
> news of salvation,
> Who says to Zion,
> 'Your God has become King' (Isa. 52.7).

Evidently Isaiah expected the imminent coming of the reign of God when all the ends of the earth would see his salvation. However, in the providence of God, the stream of that great hope was to run underground for more than five centuries until God's appointed time came. It came in the reign of the Roman Emperor Tiberius when a young man from Nazareth appeared in Galilee, proclaiming, 'The time has come; the kingdom of God is upon you; repent and believe the Gospel' (Mark 1.15 NEB). Isaiah had prophetically foreseen the time when God would really take to himself his great power and reign. 'That time,' says Jesus, 'has now arrived.' This is his 'good news'. In his person and mission—for you cannot separate message and messenger—the Reign of God is breaking decisively into history and the New Age is beginning.

This 'good news' forms the burden of all Jesus' works and words. It is the 'good news' which rings out in his sermon at Nazareth; it is the 'good news' which lies at the heart of his reply to the Baptist's question, 'Are you the one who is to come?—'the poor are hearing the good news' (Luke 7.22)—

24

and it is the 'good news' which he proclaimed to the scoffing Pharisees, 'Until John it was the law and the prophets: since then there is the good news of the kingdom of God (Luke 16.16).

In short, it was Jesus himself who first used the phrase to 'preach the gospel' of his own proclamation, and he interpreted it as a fulfilment of Isaianic prophecy. In his ministry God had begun to reign. Message and messenger were one. Jesus, the herald of the Kingdom of God, was also its bearer: he was the Reign of God incarnate.

But you cannot read far in the story of his earthly ministry till you find that Jesus' 'good news' also carries at its heart 'bad news', that the Gospel of the Kingdom of God involves a Cross. If the Reign of God is to come 'with power' we learn, it can only come through the death of the herald who calls himself the Son of Man. How are we to tie Jesus' 'good news' and 'bad news' together? Where is it laid down that the Reign of God means suffering and death for him who is the bearer of the Kingdom? Once again we find the answer in the Isaianic prophecies. If the word 'gospel' as Jesus used it, and the message of the Reign of God as he preached it, have their roots in Isa. 40 and 52, where else shall we look for 'the word of the Cross' but in Isa. 53, that prophetic song about the servant of the Lord who was to bring sinners weal by his woe, salvation by his suffering and death? The Jews themselves had found in Isaiah's Servant the suffering righteous nation. Jesus, proclaiming the Gospel in terms of Isaiah, found in the prophecy of Isa. 53, not to be separated from the Gospel, his own destiny and death—death which, under Roman rule, could only mean a Cross.

The 'gospel' originally proclaimed by Isaiah of Babylon, Jesus made his own. In his life and death and Resurrection it came true. The message and the messenger were one. And this is why the disciples, hearing his 'good news', left all and followed him.

8. The Workshop Sayings

(Mark 6.3)

'Is not this the carpenter?' So the people of 'his own country' (Nazareth) greeted Jesus whom, not so many years before, they must often have seen plying saw, plane, axe, hammer and chisel as he made ploughs, yokes, benches, boxes, coffins and perhaps boats. He may well have helped to build houses, for the Greek *tektōn* can mean 'builder' as well as worker in wood. We should therefore expect that those years when

> The Carpenter of Nazareth
> Made common things for God

would have coloured his speech and left their traces in the Gospel records.

And so it proves. The little parable of The Splinter and the Plank (Matt. 7.3-5) must recall days when, in a room strewn with planks, somebody 'got something in his eye'—a *karphos* i.e. a little chip of shaving—and work was stopped until the offending object was removed. Nor is it unlikely that, having helped to erect a house, Jesus knew from experience the wisdom of building on rock, the folly of building on sand (Matt. 7.24-27). He may even have seen just such a sand-based house shake and shudder when 'the rains came, the floods rose and the winds blew on it' before it was swept away in the 'spate'. At any rate it was on *rock* that he proposed to build the house of his Church (Matt. 16.18).

Perhaps the most humanly revealing parable from the Nazareth workshop is that of The Apprenticed Son hidden away in the fifth chapter of St. John's Gospel:

'Truly, truly I tell you, a son can do nothing by himself; he only does what he sees his father doing: what the father does the son does. For the father loves the son and shows him all he himself is doing' (John 5.19-20a).

The Jews had attacked Jesus for 'working', i.e. healing men like the cripple of Bethesda, on the sabbath day, 'My Father has never yet ceased his work,' he replied, 'and I am working too.' They retorted that by calling God his own Father he was making himself equal to God. Now according to the rabbis it was a *rebellious* son who was said to 'make himself equal to his father'. Jesus repudiates the charge: so far from being a rebel, the soul of his sonship is obedience, and he tells a parable which must go back to the Nazareth workshop days. 'Think,' he says, 'of a son apprenticed to his father's trade. (Such an arrangement must have been common in the simple society of Palestine.) He does not hammer or chisel away on his own untutored impulse. Rather he watches his father at work and copies his every action. And, in turn, the affectionate father initiates his son into all the tricks of the trade. Just so I imitate my heavenly Father, doing what he does.'

Justin Martyr, a famous second century champion of the Faith, tells us that it was ploughs and yokes that Jesus made. Both figure in his recorded words. 'No man,' he said once to a would-be disciple, 'who sets his hand to the plough, and then keeps looking back, is fit for the kingdom of God' (Luke 9.62). The secret of true discipleship, like that of good ploughing, is a firm, quiet 'holding to it', with no backward glancing.

But the finest of the workshop sayings is the ' great invitation' of Matt. 11.27-30: 'Come to me all whose work is hard, whose load is heavy; and I will give you relief. Bend your necks to my yoke and learn from me . . . for my yoke is good to bear, my load is light.' (NEB).

A yoke is a wooden frame laid over the neck of two beasts of burden, putting them in double harness and so enabling them to do together what neither by itself could do. Often in Israel's history the yoke had been a symbol of subjection. But when Jesus invites ' Yoke up with me' it is not so. ' What you cannot do by yourself,' he says, ' you can do along with me.'

What all this means we may discover if we take another look at the whole great saying in Matt. 11.25-30. To those burdened by the Law's demands he promises ' relief '; and for the heavy loads laid on them by the scribes and Pharisees (Matt. 23.4) he promises his own ' kindly ' one, the yoke of a Kingdom in which ' Abba, Father ' is sovereign, and the ' rest ' which is the peace of that new relationship with God which he knows himself uniquely qualified to mediate—for:

> No one knows the Son but the Father,
> And no one knows the Father but the Son
> And those to whom the Son may choose to reveal him.

Here is still the deepest secret of the Christian life. To all those today ' whose work is hard, whose load is heavy,' who struggle under trials and tribulations and cannot cope with the problems which life holds for them, the secret is to do it together—together with Christ. In the words of J. C. Shairp, ' we have a life in Christ to live ' and the way to do it is to accept his invitation:

> Come unto me and rest,
> Believe me, and be blest.

9. Scandals and Scandalisers

(*Mark* 9. 42-48)

According to the AV, Jesus said, ' If thine eye offend thee, pluck it out ' (Mark 9.47) and Paul asked, ' Who is offended, and I burn not ? ' (2 Cor. 11.29). But in the course of the three and a half centuries since the AV was made, the word ' offend ' has lost much of its original Latin meaning of ' strike against.' Nowadays it means simply ' displease.' We may be quite sure that when Jesus said, ' If your eye offend you,' and Paul, ' Who is offended ? ' they meant something much more serious. ' Offend ' represents the Greek *skandalizein* (30 times, in the NT) and ' offence,' *skandalon* (15 times). But in the Bible's way of it to be ' scandalised ' is like what happens when you step on a rake—something gets up and hits you !—and an ' offence ' is much more than a source of displeasure—it is something that puts you right out of your stride and brings you down on your face. (We may think of what the modern footballer does when he puts in his foot to stop a Pele or a Best.)

Skandalon and *skandalizein* were originally hunter's words. The *skandalon* was the bait-stick of a trap, then the trap itself; and to ' scandalise ' was to ' ensnare ' or ' trip up.' Always the Greek words contained the idea of the unexpected, as of course they involved the idea of a fall.

'Stumbling block' and 'cause to stumble' are the basic meanings. But when you try to turn the Greek words into English you must pay regard to the context and choose the English word which best suits it (since in no two languages are two words always precisely equivalent). Here, in my judgment, the men who made the NEB have faced the problem and solved it with much success. Take three examples. In Mark 9.47 they render Jesus' saying ' If your eye leads you astray' ('ensnare' in the sense of leading into mischief). In Jn. 6.61 when his followers are dumbfounded by Jesus' 'eucharistic doctrine,' Jesus replies, 'Does this shock you?' and in 1 Cor. 8.13 Paul says, 'If food be the downfall of my brother, I will never eat meat any more.'

It is well known that Jesus had very stern words for those who 'trapped' or 'ensnared' little ones. 'Better,' he said, 'for a man to be thrown into the sea with a millstone round his neck.' (Mark 9.42). Warnings like these (Mark 9.42-48, Matt. 18.6-9 and Luke 17.1-2) must have printed themselves indelibly on the memories of disciples who first heard him utter them. Paul was not one of these, but a verse like Rom. 14.13 suggests that he knew what Jesus said: 'Never put . . . a stumbling-block in the way of a brother '. Not only is the immediate context shot through with echoes of Jesus' teaching, but, as C. H. Dodd says[1], *skandalon* 'is not a good (i.e. classical) or usual Greek word, and the very fact that Paul uses it suggests that he knew it in the tradition of the sayings of Jesus.'

[1] *Romans*, 218.

The principle of not 'scandalising' a weaker brother—albeit a negative one—has an important place in New Testament ethics. It meant much to our Lord, and Paul in chapters like 1 Cor. 8 and Rom. 14 applies it with insight and power, showing how true he is, here as elsewhere, to 'the mind of Christ' (1 Cor. 2.16).

It only remains to add, by way of postscript, that in the Gospels it is sometimes hard to decide whether a saying about 'scandalising' children or little ones is to be taken quite literally or understood of disciples. (Jesus had memorable things to say about little children, but he was also wont to address his disciples as 'children'.) But whether he had children or humble believers in view, his warnings have not lost their relevance for Christians in the twentieth century. To 'scandalise'—to cause the downfall of either—is, for Christ, sin of the gravest sort.

10. A Ransom for Many

(*Mark* 10.45)

There is no more precious saying of Jesus in Mark's Gospel than this: 'For the Son of Man also did not come to be served but to serve and to give his life as a ransom for many (*lutron anti pollōn*)'. Spoken on the road to Jerusalem when Jesus was 'dwelling in his passion', it gave his perplexed disciples a luminous hint of the whole purpose of his mission and death.

Yet down the centuries few sayings of Jesus have been more mishandled by commentators and critics. The early Church Fathers, fastening on the word 'ransom' and straining the metaphor to its limits, debated endlessly 'To whom was the ransom paid?' ('To the devil,' said some. Others said, 'To God.') So theories of atonement were built, as they never should be, on a single text and metaphor. In

30

modern times liberal scholars (like Hastings Randall), evidently loth to believe that Jesus could have such a tremendous claim, have sought to deny it to him altogether. It is, they have said, a secondary variant of Luke 22.27 ('I am among you as one who serves') which, because it says not a word about a redemptive death, must therefore be original. A curiously *a priori* and perverse comment on one who 'came to seek and to save that which was lost.' (Luke 19.10)! Alternatively, they have dismissed it as a 'Paulinism' from the pen of Mark. The false assumption here is that Paul's was the one creative mind in the early Church and that he infected the earliest evangelist (and not him only!) with his own peculiar brand of redemptive theology. More recently one or two critics have tried to sever the saying from the OT passage which affords the clearest clue to Jesus' meaning —Isaiah's great song of the Suffering Servant.

Yet the authenticity of the saying is as undoubted as its rootage in Isaiah 53. Jesus the Son of Man (a cryptic name for the Messiah) has come 'to serve'—to be the Lord's Servant of Isaiah's prophecy, and his death, which is the climax of his mission, is that offering of his life for the 'many' (a Hebrew way of saying 'all') prophesied in Isa. 53.10-12. 'Ransom' (*lutron*) probably corresponds to the Hebrew *asham* (sin offering)[1] in vs. 10, as 'for many' echoes the triple reference to 'the many' in vss. 11 and 12.

What light does the saying shed on Jesus' thought about his death? The least his words can mean is that the suffering Son of Man is laying down his life vicariously that others may live. But it is not unduly pressing Jesus' words to say that by reason of their sins the lives of the many had become forfeit and that Jesus knew himself, as the messianic servant of the Lord, called to release them, by his death, from the doom which overhung them. 'Truly,' the Psalmist had written (Ps. 49.7f.), 'No man can ransom himself or give to God the price of his life; for the ransom of his life is costly.' What 'the many' cannot do for themselves, Jesus, by his representative and redemptive suffering, will do for them. The sacrifice of the innocent one will exempt the guilty.

[1] J. Jeremias, *The Servant of God,* 99.

Because he takes the saying seriously and, at the same time, preserves the mystery of

Desperate tides of the whole great world's anguish
Forced through the channels of a single heart,

James Denney[1] is our greatest commentator here:

'A ransom is not wanted at all except where life has been forfeited, and the meaning of the sentence unambiguously is that the forfeited lives of "the many" are liberated by the surrender of Christ's life, and that to surrender his life to do them this incalculable service was the very soul of his calling. If we find the same thought in St. Paul we shall not say that the evangelist was Paulinized but that St. Paul has sat at the feet of Jesus. And if we feel that such a thought carries us suddenly out of our depth—that, as the words fall on our minds, we seem to hear the plunge of the lead into fathomless waters—we shall not for that imagine that we have lost our way. By these things men live, and wholly therein is the life of our spirit. We cast ourselves on them because they outgo us; in their very immensity, we are assured that God is in them.'

11. Whose is the Image?

(*Mark* 12.13-17)

'Next they sent to him some Pharisees and some Herodians to catch him out in what he said. These came and said to him, "Master, we know you are an honest man, that you are not afraid of anyone, because a man's rank means nothing to you, and that you teach the way of God in all honesty. Is it permissible to pay taxes to Caesar or not? Should we pay, yes or no?" Seeing through their hypocrisy he said to them, "Why do you set this trap for me? Hand me a denarius and let me see it." They handed him one and he

[1] *The Death of Christ*, 45.

said, "Whose head is this? Whose name?" "Caesar's," they told him. Jesus said to them, "Give back to Caesar what belongs to Caesar—and to God what belongs to God." This reply took them completely by surprise.' (Jerusalem Bible).

Of all Jesus' 'Pronouncement Stories' recorded in the Gospels this is perhaps the best known—and the most misunderstood. The common error has been to regard it as a kind of judgment of Solomon which neatly separates Church and State—religion and politics—into their own spheres and provides dominical warrant for the doctrine of the 'two realms'—a doctrine which in history has sometimes led to the dangerous conclusion of the absolute right of the State to be a law to itself. In fact, while recognising that obligations due to the State are within the divine order, Jesus held that the claims of God are paramount. (Mark 12.28-31).

The setting of the story is familiar; the trap was set by Pharisees and Herodians, a most unusual alliance which would either discredit or imperil Jesus. If he answered Yes, Jesus would disgust the people who groaned under the burdens of Roman taxation. If he answered No, he was in serious trouble with the Romans. On which horn of the dilemma would he impale himself?

'Fetch me a denarius,' he replies. (The denarius was a little silver coin with the head of the Emperor Tiberius on it, and around it the legend, 'Tiberius Caesar Augustus, son of the divine Augustus.') When they produce it he asks, 'Whose head is this? Whose name?' They reply, 'Caesar's.' Then Jesus pronounces, 'Give back to Caesar what belongs to Caesar.' He refers his questioners to a decision which they had in fact reached long ago. Did they not go about their business jingling Caesar's money in their pockets, being roused to wrath only when the demand to pay Caesar's poll-tax was delivered at their door? But in fact, 'Give back to Caesar what belongs to Caesar' is only the first half of Jesus' pronouncement, and it is the second part which carries the whole weight. The question about the imperial poll-tax Jesus regards as settled long ago. The question is, What does he mean by 'Give back to God what belongs to God'?

If we answer 'The coin belongs to Caesar, but you belong

to God' we are on the right track. But we must go further, for Jesus' point is more particular and specific. The idea of the coinage is the nerve of his argument and the real parallel to the denarius—the coin used in paying the imperial poll-tax—is *man* who bears the image of God.

In her play *The Man Born to be King* Dorothy Sayers makes Jesus say to his questioners, 'You are men—and the image stamped on you is the image of God.[1] So what do you owe him?' This points the way to the true exegesis. Jesus' unspoken argument is 'Give to Caesar the taxes that are his due. But the image that is printed on you is not Caesar's but God's; therefore you yourselves belong to God.'

Here on our Lord's lips we find the Old Testament concept of man as made in the image of God. Men are God's coinage bearing his image, and what belongs to God must be paid back to him. But this is not all. The words of Jesus' reply, so far from expressing a timeless truth, find their true historical setting against the background of his announcement of the coming of God's Kingdom. On this view, 'Render unto Caesar the things that are Caesar's becomes a temporary and transient obligation—an obligation of the interim—for, whereas the reign of Caesar passes, the reign of God, now dawning, does not pass away. It is another way of expressing his command. 'Seek first the kingdom of God,' for 'the world is passing away with all its allurements, but he who does God's will stands for evermore.' (1 John 2.17 NEB).

12. The Enacted Words of Jesus

(Mark 14.22 etc.)

Actions, we say, speak louder than words. At a deeper level, Goethe declared, 'The highest cannot be spoken, it can

[1] The Early Church Father Tertullian anticipated Dorothy Sayers: 'Give to God' he said in effect, 'what is God's—his image in man—yourself.'

only be acted.' Let us apply this truth to the messianic acts of Jesus in the Gospels—the *Gesta Christi*. But before we do so, we must supply the Old Testament background needed for understanding them.

It is well known that the prophets often acted out their predictions. Thus, to take only one instance, in the valley of Hinnom Jeremiah solemnly shattered a pitcher before a group of his fellow-countrymen, in order to predict symbolically the 'breaking' of Jerusalem (Jer. 19). More eloquently than any word his action said, 'This is what God has told me is going to happen to you, O Jerusalem.'

The Hebrew word for such an act was *ōth*; but an *ōth* was more than a mere acted parable. By his act the prophet conceived of himself as entering into the divine purpose and helping it to fulfilment. His act was an *arrabōn*—a first instalment of what was divinely impending, a little part of the coming reality as yet unseen. In short, an *ōth* was both picture and pledge of what God was purposing and would shortly bring to pass.

Sometimes the prophets' actions have been compared to the 'mimetic magic' of primitive man. In fact the two—mimetic magic and prophetic symbolism— are very different. By potent formula and gesture your magician sought to coerce the deity into doing what he wanted, e.g. sending rain in time of drought. On the other hand, the Old Testament prophet, under a deep sense of constraint, uttered a message given him from on high; and he believed that his symbolic act would be effective because it embodied the Word of God which accomplishes what he purposes and succeeds in what it is sent to do (Isa. 55.11).

To this category of symbolic action belong at least half a dozen of Jesus' actions—or practices—recorded in the Gospels. Only, since Jesus knew himself to be the bearer of God's Kingdom to men, i.e. the Messiah, we should speak, in his case, not of 'prophetic' but of 'messianic' symbolism.

One of the earliest acts of Jesus' ministry was *his appointment of twelve disciples* (Mark 3.14. Cf. John 6.70 'Did I not choose you the twelve?'). 'Twelve' is no random figure; it is the number of the tribes of Old Israel. By that act

Jesus said in effect. 'God wills, through me, to raise up a new People of God.' As soon as he noted the number of the disciples, a Jew of any spiritual penetration must have scented 'a messianic programme' in Jesus' ministry. By his choice of twelve men Jesus signified his intention to create a new Israel, a new Church.

Now pass from this single act to a whole series of actions which marked the public ministry of Jesus: *again and again Jesus entertained the outcasts of society and sat at table with the traditionally 'despised and rejected' folk in Israel.* 'When Jesus was at table in his house,' we read in Mark 2.15, 'many bad characters—tax collectors and others—were seated with him and his disciples' (NEB). It was Jesus' playing-host to the religiously unrespectable that led his critics to complain, 'Behold, a glutton and a drunkard, a friend of tax collectors and sinners' (Matt. 11.19) or, 'This fellow welcomes sinners and eats with them' (Luke 15.2 and 19.5f.). Table-fellowship, be it noted, had long been a symbol not only of close fellowship with God but also of what the good time coming—the Messianic Age—would be like. These 'At Homes' of Jesus (if we may so call them) for the spiritually and socially disinherited were therefore signs, signs more significant than words, that the Messianic Age—the Age of God's great grace and forgiveness— was now dawning. Jesus appeared as 'one who acted in God's place and summoned sinners who without him would have had to flee from God.' In his act of table fellowship he was the grace of God incarnate.

Pass now from the public ministry to what might be called paradoxically the first act in his Passion. *Jesus rode into Jerusalem mounted on an ass* (Mark 11.7ff.). The clue to this riding is to be found in Zech. 9.9. Centuries before, a seer had pictured Messiah as 'lowly and riding on an ass' (the beast of peace, as the horse was of war) adding that 'he would speak peace unto the nations and his dominion would be from sea to sea.' This prophecy Jesus now acted out, suggesting in the very home and heart of Israel that he was the Messiah, but a Messiah without arms or an army, a Messiah in the very mould of Isaiah's promised 'Prince of Peace.' It is far from certain that the huzzaing crowds or even the disciples took his full meaning. What is certain is that this manner of entry into the Holy City was not only a claim to be the Messiah but a pregnant hint of the kind of Messiah he knew himself to be.

The entry was quickly followed by another Messianic act: *Jesus cleansed the temple court of its traffickers* (Mark 11.15ff.). It is not enough to say, as some have said, that this was simply the act of a religious reformer whose soul was shocked at the shameful profanation of holy things. Jesus was fulfilling the prophecy of Mal. 3.1ff. 'The Lord whom you seek will suddenly come to his temple. But who can endure the day of his coming? For he is like a refiner's fire and like fuller's soap.' But observe what Jesus actually did on that day: he cleared a space for the Gentiles in that part of the temple's precincts known as 'the Court of the Gentiles.' It was a public act proclaiming the inalienable right of the Gentiles to a place in what he called 'his Father's house' (John 2.16). Was it not also a pledge of the time when 'the other sheep'—the scattered children of God— would be gathered into one flock under one shepherd (John 10.15f.)?

We turn last to the two messianic actions of the Upper Room. Though the first is recorded only by St. John, we need not doubt that *Jesus did, on that fateful evening, gird himself with a towel and wash his disciples' feet* (John 13.1-20). Many have read the story simply as an acted parable on the theme of the glory of service. That this is part of the truth is not in doubt. But if this were all that Jesus meant, the mysterious dialogue between him and Peter would be pointless. In fact, the footwashing is an act foreshadowing the Cross. Its main motif is cleansing, and in washing his disciples' feet Jesus is proleptically and symbolically giving them a share in his destiny as the Servant Messiah soon to suffer and die. 'If I do not wash your feet,' he tells protesting Peter, 'you are not in fellowship with me.' There is no place in his fellowship for those who are not willing to be cleansed by the 'blood' of his redemptive death.

Most famous of all is the last messianic act of Jesus when *he broke bread and took a cup* (Mark 14.22ff.). In what was a double acted parable, resembling the symbolic actions of the prophets, he likened himself to the Passover Lamb. His sacrificial death, thus symbolically prophesied, Jesus believed to be fraught with atoning virtue; his blood would seal God's New Covenant with his people and avail 'for many'. And by inviting his disciples to partake of the bread and wine, Jesus gave them 'a share in the power of the broken Christ'.

Nineteen centuries later we take and eat. No more than the first disciples may we fathom all the deep mysteries of the Saviour's Passion, for

> None of the ransomed ever knew
> How deep were the waters crossed.

But their Lord is our Lord, now risen, regnant, and present with us through the Holy Spirit, and because he 'is the same yesterday, today and for ever', still able to save and strengthen all who come to God through him.

13. *Abba*

(*Mark* 14.36)

If by some wonderful retroversion in time—like that experienced by the two Oxford dons, Miss Moberly and Miss Jourdain who, in 1901, walking in Versailles, walked back into the eighteenth century[1]—we could transport ourselves back nineteen hundred years to the Nazareth home and listen to the child Jesus and his brothers and sisters addressing Joseph and Mary, the words we would hear—with the accent on the second syllable—would be *Abba* and *Imma* (shall we say 'Dada' and Mama?') Both words are Aramaic—that Semitic speech, very like Hebrew, which was our Lord's mother-tongue. Only a very few of Jesus' original Aramaic words have survived in our Greek Gospels (one thinks of *talitha kum* 'get up, my lass' and *ephphatha* 'Be opened');

[1] See their book *An Adventure*.

38

and of them *Abba,* for reasons which will emerge in a moment, is by far the most precious.

Once only in the Gospels, in Mark's record of Jesus' prayer in Gethsemane, does *Abba* occur; but beyond doubt this Aramaic word lies hidden behind those passages where Jesus says 'Father,' 'My Father' or 'The Father.' More particularly we may affirm with confidence that in all his prayers to God—from the Great Thanksgiving (Matt. 11.25-27; Luke 10.21-22) to his prayers on the Cross (Luke 23.34,46)—Jesus used *Abba,* the every-day word he had learned, more than thirty years before, in the Nazareth home. (The sole exception —the cry of dereliction (Mark 15.34)—is hardly a real one because it is a quotation from Ps. 22.1).

Here is something quite new and of capital importance for our understanding of Jesus' person and mission.

Modern scholars, and in particular Joachim Jeremias[1] of Germany, have searched the prayer literature of ancient Judaism from end to end, to see if there is any parallel to Jesus' usage. They have found none. Not a single example of this use of *Abba* to God in prayer do these sources yield. Yet Jesus, when he prayed to God, regularly used it. How are we to account, on the one hand, for the astonishing refusal of the Jews so to address God and, on the other, for Jesus' equally astonishing preference for it?

As we have noted, *Abba* 'dear Father'—it is what the grammarians call a 'caritative'—was the word little Jewish children used at home to their human father; indeed, we are told even grown-up sons and daughters went on so addressing him. It was a colloquial, everyday, family word. Yet precisely in this fact lay its 'offence' for the Jews *vis-à-vis* the Almighty. 'God is in heaven, and thou on earth.' No pious Jew would ever have dreamt of using this homely word in prayer to the high and holy One who inhabits eternity. To do so would not merely have savoured of disrespect and irreverence; it would, as John 5.17f. shows, have been tantamount to blasphemy. The fact that Jesus did just this— addressed God as *Abba,* spoke to him with the simplicity and intimacy a child uses with his father—is remarkable testimony

[1] See his *Prayers of Jesus,* Chapter 1.

to the kind of communion he had with God, the sense of unshared sonhood of which he was conscious.

Now, to be sure, Jesus' invocation of God as *Abba* might be interpreted merely psychologically. We might see in it simply the first step in his growing apprehension of God. But how inadequate this explanation is, we may see if we turn to his Great Thanksgiving—a saying even in its Greek dress so shot through with Semitic idiom that it must be genuine:

> All things have been delivered to me by my Father,
> And no one knows the Son except the Father,
> And no one knows the Father except the Son,
> And anyone to whom the Son chooses to reveal him.
>
> (Matt. 11.27).

The plain meaning of this is that Jesus regarded this form of address to God—*Abba*—as embodying the very soul of the revelation granted him by the Father. In other words, *Abba* holds the last secret of Jesus' mission and authority. He whom the Father has granted full knowledge of God has, as the Messiah, the privilege of addressing him familiarly as a son would.

But this is not all. Turn now to Luke 11.1ff: 'Lord, teach us to pray,' say the disciples, 'as John (the Baptist) taught his disciples.' What they mean is, 'Give us a distinctive prayer which will be the hallmark of your followers.' Infinitely revealing then is Jesus' answer: 'When you pray, say Father,' i.e. *Abba*. He authorises them to do as he does— gives them a share in his sonship, empowers them to speak to the heavenly Father in the same homely, trusting way a child uses with his father. Elsewhere indeed (Matt. 18.3) Jesus even seems to say that only he who can repeat this child-like *Abba* is worthy of entrance into God's Kingdom: 'Unless you turn round and become like children (i.e. say *Abba*), you will never enter the kingdom of heaven' (NEB).

One word more. Though *Abba* underlies Jesus' words when he says 'Father' 'My Father' or 'The Father,' in the Gospels the only occurrence of the Aramaic word is in Mark

14.36. But twice in Paul's letters, when he is writing to Greek-speaking Christians who knew little or no Aramaic, he introduces this 'alien' word *Abba*. 'When we cry *Abba, Father*' he says to the Christians in Rome, 'it is the Spirit himself bearing witness with our spirit that we are children of God' (Rom. 8.15f. Cf. Gal 4.6). What does this mean? It certainly means that Jesus had so hallowed the word by his own use of it that it had to be taken over into Greek-speaking circles. But it means also that the secret which Jesus shared with his disciples in the days of his flesh had now become, after Easter and Pentecost, an 'open secret'—had become the privilege of all the 'adopted' sons of God who were members of Christ's Body, the Church. And that is why still today, thanks to Jesus, we can still lift up praying hands to the unseen crying '*Abba!* Father!'

14. This Cup

(*Mark* 14.36; *John* 18.11)

'If I were asked what has been the most powerful force in the making of history,' said Macneile Dixon[1], 'I should answer: metaphor.' The hyperbole has its truth, though we cannot stop to discuss it. Suffice it to say that metaphor is of the essence of religion and poetry, and that if you were to take the metaphors out of the Bible, its power over the human heart would melt away.

Take one example only, our Lord's use of the 'cup' metaphor in the Garden of Gethsemane, so wonderfully described in Martineau's verses:

> A voice upon the midnight air
> Where Kedron's moonlit waters stray
> Weeps forth in agony of prayer,
> "O Father, take this cup away!"

[1] *The Human Situation*, 65.

> Ah, thou, who sorrowest unto death,
> We conquer in thy mortal fray,
> And earth for all her children saith,
> "O God, take not this cup away!"

What did Jesus mean by 'this cup'! For a clue we naturally turn to Christ's Bible, to the psalmists and prophets of the Old Testament, whose language he so often made his own. Now it is an astonishing fact that out of twenty-one metaphorical uses of the word 'cup' in the Old Testament, only four have the *glad* meaning which we find in 'the shepherd psalm,' 'My cup runneth over'. All the others have a very sombre sound—are a figurative way of describing divine punishment. Let the reader turn up Ps. 11.6, Ps. 75.8, Isa. 51.17,22, Jer. 25.15ff., Ezek 23.31ff., Hab. 2.15f., and he will be left in no doubt that the 'cup' in these passages is very often the cup of God's wrath against human sin.[1]

Men have often been content to call Christ's cup in Gethsemane the cup of suffering. But such an interpretation does justice neither to Old Testament usage nor to the context of the 'cup' in Mark's story. It was the cup of the divine judgment on men's sin that Jesus as the Servant Messiah was called to drink. So closely had he betrothed himself to the human race, for better, for worse, that Jesus had to taste in all its horror the wrath of God against the sin of man. Jesus' cup was in fact 'the cup our sins had mingled.' Only such an interpretation will explain his agony in the garden— 'Horror and dismay came over him,' we read (Mark 14.33)— or the later cry of dereliction on the Cross (Mark 15.34) which marks his descent into the hell of utter separation from his Father. (Paul must have been thinking of this when he wrote: 'For our sake he made him to be sin who knew no sin' 2 Cor. 5.21).

It is to 'this cup' and the agony in the garden that the writer to the Hebrews is referring: 'In the days of his earthly life he offered up prayers and petitions, with loud cries and tears, to God who was able to deliver him from the grave'.

[1] See C. E. B. Cranfield's article in *The Expository Times*, Feb. 1948.

And he adds: 'Because of his humble submission he was heard'. (Heb. 5.7 NEB).

But was his prayer in fact 'heard?' We know that God did *not* remove the cup; Christ had to drink it to the dregs. Shall we then say that, if his prayer was not answered in the obvious way, it was in fact answered in the deeper sense, i.e. he was given strength to go through with his saving work? But if the NEB translation is right, is there not another way of interpreting the word 'heard'? We may phrase it in Peter's words on the day of Pentecost, 'God,' said the apostle, 'did not let his loyal servant suffer corruption, he raised him to life again.' (Acts 2.23ff.).

15. 'He's had it!'

(*Mark* 14.41)

According to the AV, when Jesus returned to the sleeping disciples after his agony in Gethsemane, he said, 'Sleep on now and take your rest; *it is enough;* the hour is come; behold the Son of Man is betrayed into the hands of sinners. Rise up, let us go; lo, he that betrayeth me is at hand.'

The single Greek word translated 'It is enough' is *apechei*, the third person singular of the present indicative of *apecho*, a compound of the Greek verb 'have.' Most of our later versions are content to repeat the AV's 'enough.' But this impersonal meaning for the verb is neither well supported nor does it make good sense.

Why should we not give it the meaning which it commonly bears in the Greek papyri, written about the time of Christ, which we have recovered from the rubbish dumps of old Egypt?[1] There it is a commercial formula of receipt: 'I have had the money,' 'I'm paid.' Thrice in the Sermon on the

[1] This was first suggested by the Dutch scholar de Zwaan in *The Expositor*, VI, xii, 452ff.

43

Mount when Jesus says of the hypocrites, 'They have had their reward', the verb carries this commercial sense. Moreover, this meaning would fit the second half of verse 41 in Mark 14 very well: 'the Son of Man is about to be handed over to sinners.'

We suggest then that Jesus is saying of Judas, 'He's had it' 'He's got the money' 'He's been paid.' If it be objected that we might have expected Jesus to name Judas, the answer is that there was no need. Earlier in the chapter we are told that the chief priests 'promised to give him money' (14.11). Jesus himself was not unaware what was afoot (14.18). Besides, Judas's love of money, by the testimony of John 12.6, was well known. 'He's had it' must have been intelligible to the other disciples who by now must have guessed the dark business which took Judas from the Upper Room.

If now we note that the words 'sleep on now and take your rest' go better as a question, we may translate afresh: 'Still sleeping and taking your rest? He's had it! The hour is come! The Son of Man is about to be handed over to sinners. Up and let us be going! Look, there comes my betrayer!'

'He's had the money! The hour (the supreme hour of the Passion when Jesus will 'finish' God's work on a Cross) is come.' So in unholy juxtaposition we find God and Mammon. Judas, the devil's agent (Luke 22.3, John 13.2) is nonetheless the means of enabling the Lord 'to give his life as a ransom for many' (Mark 10.45). It was the 'dirtiest money' in all history, but, in the purpose and providence of God, it had to be paid to Judas, if Jesus was to 'pay the price of sin'.

16. Christ and Rewards

(*Luke* 6.35)

Our Lord spoke about rewards—heavenly rewards—and many people have regretted that he did so. With Emerson they have held that 'the reward of a thing well done is to have done it,' and there should be an end to it. A true man should believe in virtue for virtue's sake, and all talk of reward is sub-moral. It savours of that *quid pro quo* morality—the 'contract' idea of religion—which disfigured Judaism at its worst and from which, alas, Christians have not always kept themselves free.

How shall we answer the charge that our Lord's teaching on reward (the Greek word is *misthos*) is sub-moral?

To begin with, we may argue that in a universe directed to moral ends good action or character must issue in some kind of satisfaction—indeed that in the highest ethical systems there must be such satisfactions, such rewards. The real questions are: What is to be the nature of these satisfactions or rewards? And how far are they held out as inducements—as bribes?

Submitted to these tests, Christ's doctrine has nothing to fear. It does not make the Christian life a mercenary affair. All depends, as C. S. Lewis said[1] on what you mean by rewards:

'There is the reward which has no natural connexion with the things you do to earn it, and is quite foreign to the desires that ought to accompany these things. Money is not the natural reward of love; that is why we call a man mercenary if he marries a woman for the sake of her money. But marriage is the proper reward for a real lover, and he is not mercenary for desiring it. A general who fights well in order to get a peerage is mercenary; a general who fights for victory is not, victory being the proper reward of battle as marriage is the proper reward of love. The proper rewards are not simply tacked on to the activity for which they are given, but are the activity itself in consummation.' So it is with the Christian doctrine of reward. The rewards offered by Jesus, e.g. the vision of God for the pure in heart, are simply the inevitable issue of goodness in a world ruled over by a good God.

So much by way of general answer to the charge that our

[1] In his sermon 'Weight of Glory', in *Transpositions and other Addresses*.

45

Lord's doctrine is mercenary or sub-moral. But if now we examine his teaching in some detail, we may see how inept the criticism really is. Three points may be made.

First: Jesus completely repudiates the idea of merit, i.e. all suggestion that man may have a claim as of right on a divine reward. Two parables will suffice as proof. The little story of the Farmer and his Man (Luke 17.7-10) flatly rejects any right of man to such a reward. 'We are servants,' it says, 'and deserve no credit; we have only done our duty.' The parable of the Labourers in the Vineyard (Matt. 20.1-15) which we ought to re-name 'the Good Employer', destroys the very idea of reward while engaged in using it. Each man in the story, the last come as well as the first, receives the same day's wage, a *denar*. It was this that caused all the trouble between employees and employer. The whole award seemed to the workers to represent neither strict justice nor sound economics. Precisely so, and this was of Jesus' deliberate intending. 'There is such a thing,' said T. W. Manson,[1] commenting on the parable, 'as the twelfth part of a *denar*. It was called a *pondion*. But there is no such thing as a twelfth part of the love of God.' The whole point of this tale about the Good Employer, who is God, is that the rewards of the Kingdom are to be measured not by man's desert but by God's grace—his wonderful kindness to the undeserving.

Second: Jesus promises reward to those who are obedient without thought of reward. 'Do good,' he says, 'and lend without expecting any return; and you will have a rich reward' (Luke 6.35 NEB). And in the parable of the Last Judgment (Matt. 25.31-46), sometimes called 'The Story of the Great Surprises', 'the blessed of my Father' turn out to be those who have helped and served the needy with no thought of a recompense.

Third: the reward for all is the same—the Kingdom of God—God's saving presence and fellowship here and now and divine glory hereafter. And we may add that the clear implication of the Talents parable is that the reward for a trusted servant is greater responsibility and closer fellowship with the master.

[1] *The Sayings of Jesus,* 220.

46

St. Paul once referred to 'the reward of grace' (Rom. 4.4), contrasting it with every reward of works to which men may lay claim. The phrase epitomises Christ's idea of reward. All reward, he says, is simply God's generous love. It is 'divine glory undeservedly received'. This is the new revelation of Christ, and it distinguishes Christianity from Judaism and from all other religions.

17. 'Are only a few to be saved?'

(Luke 13.23 NEB)

This is the question the theological inquisitives have always liked to ask; and not a few in Christian history have been sure they knew the answer. Burns's 'Holy Willie', in the eighteenth century, was one of them:

> 'O Thou, who in the heavens does dwell,
> Who, as it pleases best Thysel,
> Sends ane to heaven an' ten to hell,
> A' for Thy glory,
> And not for any gude or ill
> They've done afore Thee.'

To such a stanza our first Christian reaction must be, 'This cannot be God—the God and Father of our Lord Jesus Christ.' But Holy Willie might have retorted on us by quoting scripture. Did not Jesus say, 'Many are called, but few are chosen' (Matt. 22.14) and 'Narrow is the gate and strait the way that leads to life, and few are those who find it' (Matt. 7.14)? How shall we answer him?

To begin with, we may agree that Jesus never said salvation was an easy thing. To this matter we will return, but, meantime, we may point out that 'many' in Matt. 22.14 has the sense of 'all'. Jesus is not speaking primarily of God's selection by predestination (as Holy Willie was) but of the boundlessness of his invitation. God invites all men into his Kingdom.

And if 'but few are chosen' seems to support Holy Willie, we may reply that the words are best taken dialectically.[1] This is a paradox which warns us that our calling and election can never be taken for granted but stand continually under the grace and judgment of God.

But—and this is the next part of our reply—have we any right to deduce from two isolated texts a complete eschatology enabling us to fix the populations of hell and heaven on a ten to one ratio? If the matter were to be settled simply by quoting texts, we might retort that according to Jesus '*many* will come from east and west and sit at table with Abraham, Isaac and Jacob in the kingdom of heaven' (Matt. 8.11; Luke 13.29) and that he expressly said that the purpose of his dying was to 'give his life as a ransom for many'—for all (Mark 10.45).

Yet this is not the end of our answer. When the theologically curious of his day put the question to Jesus, 'Are only a few to be saved?' he replied, 'Struggle to get in through the narrow door, for I tell you that many will try to enter and not be able' (Luke 13.24 NEB). He compares the way of salvation to a door which God opens and man enters. Without God man's entry cannot be made. But once the door is open, man has to make his way in. Nor is entrance easy: it is a case of struggling rather than of strolling in; and if some fail to enter, it is not because God is unable to let them in, but because they refuse to enter on the only terms on which entrance is possible.

The truth of the matter is that Jesus turned the question of theological curiosity into an existential challenge. We have no key to the eternal destiny of others except that which we have for our own. 'Are only a few to be saved?' was the question put to him nineteen hundred years ago. Jesus' answer was, 'Few enough to make you afraid you may not be there. See to your entry.'[2]

Here is the timeless wisdom of Christ. Should it not also be a *verbum sapienti*—a word to the wise—for all his followers?

[1] K. L. Schmidt, *Theological Dictionary of the New Testament*, III, 495.

[2] P. T. Forsyth, *The Justification of God*, 55.

18. Hating and Loving

(Luke 14.26)

'If anyone comes to me,' said Jesus to a crowd of followers somewhere on the road to Jerusalem, and does not hate his own father and mother and wife and children and brothers and sisters, yes, and even his own life, he cannot be my disciple.'

The saying must have staggered them as it has staggered Christ's followers ever since. The ordinary man, reading it for the first time, takes Jesus to be saying, 'To be a follower of mine, you must hate your family.' This he thinks is more than flesh and blood can bear. How, he asks, does it square with the fifth commandment, 'Honour your father and your mother'? And is it not completely out of character in one who said, 'Thou shalt love thy neighbour as thyself,' and bade his disciples 'love their enemies'? What are we to make of it?

The first thing to remember is that our Lord's style of speech was Semitic. Now the Semite deals in extremes—light and darkness, truth and falsehood, love and hate—all primary colours and no half shades. He says 'Jacob I loved and Esau I hated' (Mal. 1.2f), not 'I loved Jacob more than Esau.' Thus when Deut. 21.15f lays down the law about a man with two wives, 'the one loved and the other hated', it means simply that the man loves one wife more than the other. In such contexts the horrid verb 'hate' means 'love less'. Any true disciple of his, says Jesus, must love his family less than himself. Look up the parallel saying in Matt. 10.37, and the meaning is clear: 'He who loves father and mother more than me is not worthy of me.' (Let us remember that there had been a day when Jesus himself had had to choose between his own family and God's cause. 'Who are my mother and brothers?' he had asked, and he had answered, 'Whoever does the will of God is my brother and sister and mother' (Mark 3.31-35).

But to say that 'hate' means 'love less' in Jesus' hard saying is not to rob it of all its hardness. It still throbs with something of the rigour and intensity that informs men's speech in time of war. 'In battle,' said the Greek poet Tyrtaeus, 'a man must count his own life his enemy and the black doom of death as dear as the beams of the sun.' Moreover, as history proclaims, the great captains—be it a Garibaldi or a Churchill[1]—have ever had a way of declaring their terms starkly and uncompromisingly to their followers. This is our second clue to our Lord's meaning.

It is no accident that in this very context Jesus speaks of the venture of discipleship as like that of a king going to war with another. For is he not spear-heading a campaign—the campaign of the Kingdom of God against the forces of darkness and the devil, a campaign which, as he knows, spells death for himself and suffering for his followers? He is going to Jerusalem to die and already he is 'dwelling in his Passion'. Can we wonder then that he requires all would-be followers to count well the cost—to put every family tie behind them—if they would enlist under his banner?

Today some men still find themselves called to 'hate' their families and brave the dark and dangerous places of the earth for the work of Christ. Let us thank God for their high heroism, and do what we can to support them. If the rest of us stay-at-home Christians are bound to 'honour' our fathers and mothers, and not 'hate' them, let us remember that we too are called to a sacrificial love for Christ's needy brethren around our own doors, and that if we fail in this we are not 'worthy of him'.

[1] 'I offer hunger, thirst, forced marches, battles and death' (Garibaldi).
'I have nothing to offer but blood, toil, tears and sweat' (Churchill).

19. 'Paradise'

(Luke 23.43)

Soldiers have a way of bringing home with them, among other things, foreign and outlandish words which soon become naturalised in the language. One such soldier, four centuries before Christ, was Xenophon, the friend of Socrates. The word Xenophon brought home from his campaigning in Persia was *pairidaeza*. Originally it meant 'garden' or 'park'. And in the course of the succeeding centuries this old Persian word achieved international circulation, appearing in Greek, Aramaic and Hebrew. When, for example, in the third and second centuries before Christ, the men who made the Greek Old Testament came to translate Gen. 2.8, 'The Lord God planted a garden in Eden', the word they used to render the Hebrew *gen* was *paradeisos*, 'paradise'.

'Paradise' occurs three times in the New Testament—first, in Christ's promise to the penitent thief, next of Paul's 'rapture' (2 Cor. 12.4), and finally in the Letter to the Church at Ephesus in the book of Revelation: 'To him who is victorious I will give the right to eat from the tree of life that stands in the Garden of God' (Rev. 2.7). Clearly in the intervening centuries our soldier's word from Persia had gathered about it quite a theology.

All began in Eden (Gen. 2). As it began with a garden, said the Hebrews, so when God has recreated and redeemed this fallen world, it will end with another Eden. (When the Day of the Lord comes, said Ezekiel, 'everyone will say, This land, so recently a waste, is now like a garden of Eden'. Ezek. 36.35).

But this is only half the story. About two centuries before Christ was born the Hebrews rose to the great belief in immortality—to the faith that the friends of God do not perish but are in his holy keeping for ever. But where? Not, as they

51

had once believed, in a dim and dreary underworld, called 'Sheol', beyond the jurisdiction of the Almighty, but in a hidden paradise prepared by God for the righteous. So 'paradise' became another name for the abode of the blessed after death.

If we ask why 'paradise' is not used oftener in the New Testament, the reason lies, as always, in 'the Fact of Christ'. It was his coming that made the conception of life after death a new thing. For was it not the heart of the Christian hope, that those who were 'in Christ' now would one day be 'with Christ' in his glory? And had not Jesus himself prayed in the Upper Room, 'Father, I desire that these men, who are thy gift to me, may be with me where I am, so that they may look upon my glory' (John 17.24)?

It is undoubtedly a very beautiful conception of life beyond death, this of 'the Garden of God'. But no less so is the Scotsman's 'Land of the Leal'. If any English reader has supposed that this is but another way of describing 'Caledonia stern and wild', let him turn up 'leal' (loyal) in Chambers's *Twentieth Century Dictionary*. Its original lexicographer was a Scotsman, but he did not lack a sense of humour. 'Land of the Leal', he says. 'Heaven, not Scotland'.

20. The Nameless Ones

(John 1.35 etc.)

What mortal discovered fire? What unknown genius invented the wheel? Whose hands raised the trilithons of Stonehenge? 'Who fished the murex up?' The story of man poses many unanswered questions. So does the story of Jesus and of the early Church. For a few examples: Who was the rich young ruler? Who first saw the risen Lord, Peter or Mary Magdalene? Who first brought the Gospel to Rome? Who wrote the Epistle to the Hebrews? The New Testament does not tell us.

Yet, as nature is said to abhor a vacuum, so the early Christians were not content with the anonymity or the silence of the scriptures. They sought to name the nameless ones. Sometimes doubtless they found help in oral tradition; sometimes they resorted to ingenious deduction; and often it must have been a matter of pious guessing—or invention.

Consider first those nameless ones for whom Christian tradition—whether preserved in apocryphal Gospels and Acts, or in the writings of Church fathers and historians, or in later Christian sources— contrived to find names. The mysterious magi were named as Gaspar, Melchior and Balthasar; the bridegroom at Cana of Galilee, John, son of Zebedee; the woman with the issue of blood, Veronica. From these same sources we learn that Christ's seventy missioners included Barnabas, Matthias and Joseph Barsabbas, that Pilate's wife was called Procula, that the two thieves crucified with Christ were Dysmas and Gestas, and that the Roman soldier who pierced his side bore the name of Longinus.

Then there are the other nameless ones at whose identity later scholars have made what we call nowadays 'educated guesses'.

Many have held that the anonymous disciple of John 1.35,40 was John, son of Zebedee, the beloved disciple. He too is thought to have been 'the other disciple' (John 18.15) who procured Peter's entry into the High Priest's courtyard—though some have doubted whether a provincial fisherman could possibly have been 'familiar friend' (*gnōstos*, John 18.15) to His Holiness the High Priest.

It is a well-known and plausible suggestion that Mark was the young man who fled naked from the garden of Gethsemane when the arresting posse laid hands on the 'linen cloth' he was wearing (Mark 14.51). Commenting on the occurrence of this trifling detail in the high drama of Christ's arrest and trial, Canon Streeter once said that it was as if a reporter today were describing a terrible railway accident—the wild confusion, the telescoped carriages, the groans of the injured and the dying—and then were to remark, 'Just then Mr. John Smith lost his pocket handkerchief'. Mark's verse is of the same sort—it is pointless unless it refers

53

to Mark himself—unless it is his own modest signature in the corner of his Gospel: his quiet way of saying, 'I was there'.

Luke, the third evangelist, has been the subject of two fascinating conjectures. In Acts 16.9 when Paul, during his second missionary journey, came to Troas (near 'the ringing plains of windy Troy') he had a dream in which he saw 'a man from Macedonia' who begged him, 'Come over and help us'. It was Sir William Ramsay who suggested that the man was Luke himself. Very conceivably Paul met him for the first time at Troas, and their talk together sowed a seed of missionary purpose in Paul's mind which came to maturity in a vivid dream. It is a point in favour of Ramsay's conjecture that the 'we' which indicates Luke's presence in the company starts straight away: 'And when he had seen the vision, immediately *we* sought to go on into Macedonia' (Acts 16.10).

In 2 Cor. 8.17 Paul tells the Corinthians that he is sending Titus to Corinth to uplift their contribution for the poor Christians in the mother Church at Jerusalem. 'With him', he continues, 'we are sending the brother whose praise in the Gospel is through all the churches'. Could 'the brother' have been the physician-evangelist? So Origen of Alexandria thought in the third century, and many since have agreed with him. If Luke was left at Philippi when Paul first visited it and stayed there till the time of his return some years later, he may well have made himself such a prime favourite with the Christians of Macedonia as to become an obvious person to collect the monies from the Gentile churches for the poor saints in Jerusalem.

Who is the 'Syzygus' of Phil. 4.3 whom Paul bids try to reconcile the two quarrelling women in the church at Philippi? The Greek word means literally 'yoke fellow'. Possibly Paul is referring to a 'colleague' unnamed, though the readers would know him. Possibly 'Syzygus' is a proper name on which Paul is punning ('Be true to your name and bring these two women together.') Yet no instance of such a proper name has been found; and perhaps the best guess is that he was Epaphroditus (his name means 'charming') who bore the letter to Philippi.

So much for speculation and inspired guessing. But how many thousands upon thousands of Christians there have been who 'have no memorial' either in the New Testament or our Church history books, yet to whom the cause of Christianity owes an incalculable debt! If on all such, as Sir Thomas Browne says, 'the iniquity of oblivion has blindly scattered her poppy', we must believe, as Origen said of the Writer to the Hebrews, that they are known to God and that 'their names are in the book of life'.

21. The Gospel within the Gospels

(John 3.16)

'God so loved the world that he gave his only Son, that whosoever believes in him should not perish but have eternal life'. (RSV).

Many consider this the greatest verse in the New Testament. Better than any other it sums up the meaning of the blessed thing God did when he gave men Jesus. 'The Gospel within the Gospels' was Luther's name for it.

All began, St. John says, in the loving will of God, and took effect in the gift of his only Son to the world. Perhaps, as he wrote, John thought (as Paul did in Rom. 8.32) of Abraham in the land of Moriah. What the patriarch had once, at the divine bidding, stood ready to do, the Almighty himself had done: 'He gave his only Son'. And if we ask whether 'gave' refers to the Incarnation or to the Cross, the answer surely is: 'both'.

St. John's aorist (or past) tense here is to be noted. It is the finest example in the New Testament of the theological value of Greek grammar. The Greek *hōste* 'so that' may be followed either by an infinitive or by an indicative. The evangelist might have written *hōste dounai*—'so as to give', to mark the measure of the potential gift. Instead, he chose to write *hōste edōken* 'so that he gave'—to declare the magnitude of the recorded act. For the gospel is not the propagation of an idea, however sublime, like 'God is love'; it is the proclamation of a deed of God in the stuff of history which for us men made the decisive difference between death and life. 'That whoever believes in him should not perish'. Who shall fathom all the depth of this sombre-sounding word 'perish'? Yet it certainly implies that a man, by his sinning, may die out of God's favour (which is 'life') irrevocably and for ever. From such a doom God has designed to deliver men by the gift of his Son who is the Life and the Way to Life (John 11.25, 14.6).

'Life eternal' (*zoē aioniōs*) is 'the life of the Age to Come', the New Order of God which has come with the coming of Christ. It is not simply 'everlasting life' (as the AV has it) —a mere 'going on for ever', like Tennyson's 'Brook'. It is life of a new quality, life lived in communion with God through Christ, life with the tang of eternity about it, life reproducing in its possessors God's own self-giving love, life that can never die because it is God's own life. And to accept this gift of God by faith in Christ his Son—by putting one's whole allegiance in him—is to be a Christian.

'To have part in the divine life of Jesus Christ', said Emil Brunner[1], 'to stand in the midst of history and be comprehended in eternal salvation, through the reconciliation made in him who is called the Life and the Way to Life, this is to be a Christian—to have life eternal'.

'All this and heaven too'.

[1] *The Theology of Crisis,* 67.

22. 'Jesus wrote'

(John 8.6 A.V.)

The story of Jesus and the adulteress is one of the best-known Gospel stories, and yet, in a sense, is not a Gospel story at all. Consider what our various versions do with it. If the Jerusalem Bible, like the Authorised Version, puts the story at the beginning of the 8th chapter of John's Gospel, it adds: 'The author of this passage is not John; the oldest MSS do not include it, or place it elsewhere.' The Revised Standard Version relegates it to a footnote. The New English Bible puts it in an appendix at the end of John's Gospel. All this seems very summary and shoddy treatment for a story which for most readers has all the ring of truth and authenticity about it. How did it originate?

About the beginning of the second Christian century Papias the Church father knew a story about a woman accused of many sins (later writers said 'adultery') before the Lord. This was probably our one. It is one of those tales about Jesus which was current in the Church's oral tradition, a tale which some Christian scribes evidently believed ought to have found a place in the canonical Gospels. So some put it at the beginning of John's 8th chapter because it seemed to illustrate Jesus' saying, 'I judge no one' (John 8.15). Others thought its proper place was at Luke 21.38, because it locates Jesus on the Mount of Olives. Here we need go no further into the evidence of the MSS. Enough to say that scholars agree, on the one hand, that textual evidence shows the story was not an original part of the Fourth Gospel, and, on the other hand, it preserves a genuine incident in the life of Jesus, no doubt belonging to his final ministry in Jerusalem when his enemies were trying to trap him.

Our interest here is that this is the only occasion on which we hear of Jesus writing—not with a pen but with his finger, on the ground. Why, and what was he writing?

One suggestion is that he was scribbling almost mechanically on the ground with his finger to cover his embarrassment at the whole sorry spectacle before his eyes. He was, as we would say, 'doodling', in order to conceal his burning sense of shame at sin being made the excuse by so-called religious men to further their own wicked purposes.

A second suggestion depends on taking the Greek verb for 'wrote' *(kategraphen)* in the sense of 'register' (a sense it could undoubtedly bear) and 'earth' *(gen)* in the sense of 'dust'. Jesus was 'registering' the accusation of the scribes and Pharisees 'in the dust', so that there might be no permanent record of it. But if the stress were really being laid on the phrase 'in the dust', we should have expected not 'earth' but the usual Greek word for 'dust', which is *konia*.

But the likeliest suggestion, in our view, is that which makes Jesus here ironically play the part of Roman judge.

Like the story of the Tribute Money (Mark 12.13-17), this is a tale of a trap set for Jesus by the scribes and Pharisees. If Jesus sanctions the stoning of the adulteress, he usurps the power of Rome who alone could inflict capital punishment. If he forbids it, he contravenes the law of Moses which prescribed death for an adulteress (Lev. 20.10). But, as with the Tribute Money, Jesus adroitly avoided the trap—by writing with his finger on the ground.

Now this writing of his accorded with the procedures of Roman law. In a Roman court the presiding judge would first write down the sentence on a tablet, before getting up to read it aloud. This is what Jesus did. By his action he said in effect, 'You are inviting me to play the judge in true Roman fashion. Very well, I will do so.' Stooping down, he pretends to write the sentence on the ground, after which he straightens up and reads it out: 'Let the man who is without sin among you,' he says, 'cast the first stone at her.' ('The hands of the witnesses' we read in Deut. 17.7, 'shall be first upon him to put him to death.')

It is a master-stroke of mercy seasoning justice. Jesus defeats the plotters by 'going through the motions' of passing sentence, but at the same time so wording the sentence that it cannot be carried out. He does not condone the woman's sin—'Go and sin no more'—but neither does he condemn the woman,—'neither do I condemn you'.

St. Paul once bade his readers note the 'magnanimity' of Christ (2 Cor. 10.1). His Greek word *epieikeia* describes the man who knows how to relax justice and let mercy come in. The story of the adulteress perfectly illustrates it. Jesus does not condone the woman's sin—this is the justice of Jesus. He refuses to condemn the sinner,—this is his mercy. And it is this delicate balancing of justice and mercy which makes this one of the immortal stories about Jesus.

Robert Burns once counselled:

> Then gently scan your brother man,
> Still gentler sister woman,
> Though they may gang a kennin wrang,
> To step aside is human.

But 'gentle scanning' of 'sister woman' is, by Jesus' judgment, also divine, even if Jesus does not 'step aside'—ignore the sin. In our day it often falls to Christians to sit in judgment on men and women who, in one way or another, sully the sanctity of the marriage bond. It there not a plain hint in this story for all such Christian administrators of justice that the strictly legalistic administraion of laws, however lofty the ideals they may embody, is not, in the last resort, the best way of dealing with sinners as persons? More especially as not even the best of us is 'sinless'?

59

23. The Glory of God

(John 13.31)

When Humpty Dumpty said, 'There's glory for you' and explained to a mystified Alice that he really meant, 'There's a nice knock-down argument for you', he went on to say, rather scornfully, 'When I use a word, it means just what I choose it to mean, neither more nor less'.

The New Testament Greek word for 'glory' is *doxa*. In classical Greek it meant 'opinion'—what a man himself thinks —and then what others think of him, 'reputation'—especially good repute, in one word 'honour'. But when you study the glory of God in the New Testament, you might almost think the writers had used the word 'glory' with Humpty Dumpty's sovereign freedom, pouring into it meanings which would have made a classical Greek stare and gasp. And thereby hangs a Hebrew tale.

The Hebrew word for 'glory' is *kabōd*. 'Weight' was its original meaning, but it came to signify 'worth', 'wealth', 'power', 'dignity', 'majesty', etc., and—in a secondary sense —the 'honour' accorded to 'worth', whether human or divine.

The earliest Hebrews probably conceived of God's glory meteorologically. As the thunder was God's voice, the lightning was his manifested power. And something of this idea of radiance or splendour seems to cling to their later and higher concepts of God's glory. Brightness, as of the rainbow in the cloud, is a dominant element in Ezekiel's vision of God's glory (Ezek. 1.28). But as the Hebrews advanced in their knowledge of God, they got beyond the mere idea of brightness. It was the majesty of God revealed in his creation which was in the Palmist's mind when he sang, 'The heavens declare the glory of God' (Ps. 19.1). And Isaiah of Jerusalem's inaugural vision shows how they moralised their concept of God's glory, came to think of it as his

60

manifested holiness and purity. 'Woe is me, for I am undone,' cries the prophet when he discerns the glory of God in the temple, 'for I am a man of unclean lips, and I dwell in the midst of a people of unclean lips; for my eyes have seen the King, the Lord of hosts.' (Isa. 6.5).

For the Hebrews, then, the glory of God meant his manifested power, splendour, majesty and holiness, and we find their later prophets looking forward to a supreme disclosure of God's glory in the good time coming, the Messianic Age—

'God in his glory shall appear
When Sion he builds and repairs' (Ps. 102.16).

and the prophet announces to Jerusalem the dawning of that eternal day, 'Arise, shine, for your light has come, and the glory of the Lord has risen upon you.' (Isa. 60.1).

For the next chapter in the story of *doxa* and *kabōd* we go to Alexandria where in the centuries just before Christ's coming the Old Testament was turned into Greek—became what we call the Septuagint. Why did the Jews in Alexandria who made the translation choose to render the Hebrew *kabōd* by the Greek *doxa*? In the subjective sense of 'honour' the two words overlapped. Either then they assumed that *doxa* like *kabōd*, meant both 'majesty' (objective) and 'honour' (subjective), or 'they simply decided to pay *doxa* extra and make it work overtime' (G. B. Caird). In any case, it was a momentous decision. The Greek word was immediately dyed with Hebrew meaning. At once it acquired the wealth of theological significance that had gathered round the Hebrew word. A word which for Greeks like Plato had meant 'opinion' or 'reputation' came to express the majesty and mercy of God.

So to the New Testament. Its writers—all Jews with the exception of Luke—read their scriptures, for the most part, in the Septuagint translation, and inevitably their Greek was stained with Hebrew meaning. In other words, for them the glory of God meant not God's 'opinion' but his manifested power and splendour and holiness. Yes, but now—and this is the heart of the New Testament Gospel—the Messianic Age has dawned, the Kingdom of God has been inaugurated

61

with Christ's coming and with the advent of the Spirit, and 'glory' is both realised,—

> The men of grace have found
> Glory begun below—

and still to be expected in the future when God completes his saving work in Christ.

Accordingly, in the New Testament, Christ who is in fact the Kingdom, the saving sovereignty of God, in action, is presented as the glory of God made visible on earth to men who have eyes to see it. In so far as God's glory is his manifested power, the key to that power is to be found in the 'mighty acts' that make up the Gospel story. In so far as the glory of God stands for the manifested divine splendour, we see that splendour 'in the face of Christ' (2 Cor. 4.6), and Christ can even be called 'the glory', the Shekinah, of God (Jas. 2.1). And in so far as a state of light is the final destiny of God's people (Rom. 8.18; 1 Cor. 15.43; 1 Peter 5.1), that light derives its meaning from Christ 'the Lord of glory'.

But perhaps it was given to St. John to see deepest into the glory of God as revealed in Christ. If for John Christ's 'signs' manifest his glory (John 2.11)—which is God's—the Cross is the sign *par excellence,* the supreme disclosure of God's glory. Consider what Jesus says in the Upper Room after the traitor Judas has gone out on his dark mission, 'Now is the Son of Man glorified, and God is glorified in him' (John 13.31). The 'now' is the hour of Jesus' death when he will give them a final token of his love, and Jesus speaks of it as if it were already an accomplished fact. What his words mean can be paraphrased thus: 'Now the Son of Man has been invested with divine glory and God has revealed his glory in him.' The Cross is the place where Divine glory is supremely shown. A crucified man is the burning focus of God's glory.

At Calvary then, according to St. John, God is saying to us, 'There's glory for you—what I mean by glory.' Divine glory is divine love—the love of God suffering in Christ for the sins of the world, even unto death. It is because Christians have seen the Cross like this that they have responded from St. Paul onwards, 'In the Cross of Christ I glory' or cried with Isaac Watts:

> Love so amazing, so divine,
> Demands my soul, my life, my all.

24. 'Many Mansions'

(John 14.2)

Our modern translators agree that the AV's 'mansions' no longer happily translates the Greek *monai,* for the simple reason that nowadays the word 'mansions' suggests a stately home in England, and, north of the Border, 'a big hoose'. Yet we should wrong the men who made the AV if we attributed their translation to a grandiose taste in heavenly residences.

In its origin the Latin *mansio,* like the Greek *monē,* is 'a remaining place.' But the word developed a special meaning on the mediaeval stage where 'mansions' were the separate apartments representing heaven, earth and hell. It is this usage that explains the AV's 'mansions': the translators were not dreaming of stately homes in heaven.

But if not 'mansions' what? Some, like William Temple, have taken *monai* to mean 'halting-places' in the next world —wayside caravanserais in the soul's journey to God. When therefore our Lord says, 'I am going to prepare the way for you' he is presenting himself as 'our spiritual dragoman' who goes ahead to make arrangements for us who follow him.

It is an attractive suggestion as old as Origen, the greatest Biblical scholar of antiquity. If we cannot accept it, the reason is to be found in the twenty-third verse of this same chapter. 'If a man loves me,' says Jesus, 'he will keep my word, and my Father will love him, and we will come to him and make our *monē* with him.' Here *monē* cannot mean a temporary halt; it must mean a permanent abode.

So in John 14.2 the meaning must be 'abodes' (Moffatt), 'dwelling places' (NEB), 'rooms' (RSV). 'Abode' nowadays has a slightly archaic ring about it. The NEB's rendering finds beautiful illustration in the second paraphrase:

> And in God's house for evermore
> My dwelling-place shall be.

But the RSV's 'rooms' is briefest and perhaps best.

25. Comforter or Advocate?

(John 16.7)

Four times in St. John's Gospel (14.16, 26; 15.26; 16.7) the Holy Spirit—also named 'the Spirit of truth'—who is to serve as Christ's *alter ego* after he has returned to the Father, is called 'the Paraclete' (Gr. *paraklētos*). 'Comforter' is the AV's translation. But our modern translators will have none of it. One or two (like Moffatt) plump for 'Helper'; but most prefer 'Advocate'. What ails them at the time-honoured translation? Why have they preferred a word which smacks of the law-court?

'Comforter' (from the Latin *confortator)* originally meant 'Strengthener'. But in the centuries which have elapsed since the AV was made, the word 'comfort' has somehow gone soft. 'All modern comforts' we say, hinting at cosiness; and we bestow the name 'comforter' on objects from woollen scarves to babies' 'dummies'.

Yet this is only half the explanation. Etymologically, the Greek *paraklētos,* a passive form from *parakaleō,* suggests 'the AA man'. It means 'one called to the side of another', to aid or to advise. But since the word's usual background is not a highway but a law-court, the normal meaning is the 'advocate' of a party or cause, and particularly the advocate for the defence. This is how it is generally used in classical Greek, in the Apostolic Fathers, and even among the Jewish rabbis who borrowed the word from the Greeks. Only when we come to the later Greek Fathers do we find the word acquiring the active sense of 'encourager' or 'consoler'.

But there are good theological reasons as well as philological ones for changing from 'Comforter' to 'Advocate'. We know, for example, that the Jews thought of the Holy Spirit in this juridical way. In the *Testaments of the Twelve Patriarchs,* a Pharisaic work of about 100 B.C., we read that 'the Spirit of truth *bears witness* and *accuses* of everything so that the sinner is set on fire in his heart and cannot lift his face to his *judge*'. And in the Dead Sea Scrolls 'the Spirit of truth' is the 'advocate' of 'the children of light' in their struggle against 'the children of darkness'. In both Jewish sources juridical language is pressed into the service of religion—just as Paul employs law-court words like 'justify' (acquit) and 'justification' (acquittal) to express the heart of his Gospel—God's free forgiveness of sinners for Christ's sake.

With all this in mind we may now return to our four passages in the Fourth Gospel where the Holy Spirit is called 'the Paraclete'.

In the first two there is nothing specifically juridical about the Spirit's work. His role is to indwell Christ's disciples, teaching them and reminding them of all that he had said. He is to be Indweller and Remembrancer. But in the third he is to 'bear witness' to Christ, and the fourth is thoroughly juridical:

Still I must tell you the truth:

It is for your good that I am going
because unless I do,
the Advocate will not come to you;
but if I do go,
I will send him to you.

And when he comes,
he will show the world how wrong it was,
about sin,

and about who was in the right,
and about judgment:
about sin:
proved by their refusal to believe in me;
about who was in the right:
proved by my going to the Father
and your seeing me no more;
about judgment:
proved by the prince of this world being already condemned
(John 16.7-11. Jerusalem Bible.)

Here clearly the Spirit is not one who 'comforts' in sickness or sorrow. He is the Advocate (or, as the RSV has it, using the word in its American spelling and sense, 'Counselor'). As somebody has put it, he is not Doctor Kildare but Perry Mason, with this difference however that Perry Mason appears (or used to appear) as Counsel for the defence, whereas the Paraclete here is Counsel for the prosecution, with 'the world' standing in the dock.

What relevance, may we ask, has this juridical language about the Spirit for us today? 'The world'—that is, all the forces that are indifferent or hostile to the Church of Christ —is still with us. In such a setting the Paraclete still exercises his ministry among us; and the only way by which 'the world' can learn that the death of Christ was not the end, is that the Spirit which indwelt Jesus is still at work among his followers today wherever, by sacrificial living or by courageous witness or by 'Christian action', they testify to their Lord's living power and reality.

26. The Gospel Hyperboles

(John 21.25 etc.)

'Hyperbole' is a Greek word meaning 'excess' which occurs eight times in Paul's letters. For us nowadays it stands for a figure of speech—extravagant speech. When St. John, for

66

Review Copy

EXPLORING THE NEW TESTAMENT

by

A. M. Hunter

Paper — 50p.

Publication Date

18th May, 1971.

We have pleasure in submitting this book for review and should be glad to receive two copies of any notice which may appear in your journal.

We request that no review of this book should appear before publication date.

SAINT ANDREW PRESS
121 GEORGE STREET EDINBURGH

example, ends his Gospel with the words 'There are also many other things which Jesus did; were everyone of them to be written, I suppose that the world itself could not contain the books that would be written,' he indulges in pardonable hyperbole—pardonable because hyperbole deliberately exaggerates for the sake not of deception but of emphasis.

There is a time and place for everything; and no doubt the precisians who insist on measured accuracy on every occasion have their uses in this world. But the men who have produced great literature have ever trafficked in hyperboles. When Shakespeare makes Macbeth ask,

> Will all great Neptune's ocean wash this blood
> Clean from my hand?   No, this my hand will rather
> The multitudinous seas incarnadine,
> Making the green one red,

or Isaac Watts declares (in what Arnold pronounced the greatest hymn in the English language),

> Were the whole realm of nature mine
> That were an offering far too small

their hyperboles, by appealing to the imagination (which William Blake thought another name for the Holy Ghost), move us as no matter-of-fact statement would.

But this splendid 'excess' in speech also marks the great popular teachers. We men seem to be so made that plain, precise statements of truth leave us cold and unmoved. Hyperbole is needed to arrest our attention, to 'stab us broad awake', to drive home truth. No one knew this better than our Lord himself. 'Every now and then,' says R. L. Stevenson[1], 'Jesus quits the beaten track to pioneer the unexpressed, and throw out a pregnant and magnanimous hyperbole; for it is only by some bold poetry of thought that men can be strung up above the level of every-day conceptions to accept some higher principle of conduct.' Consider our Lord's words about the danger of wealth: 'It is easier for a camel to go through the eye of a needle than for a rich man to enter the Kingdom of God' (Mark 10.25). If

[1] *The Pocket R.L.S.*, 129.

only commentators had remembered Jesus' 'bold poetry of thought', they would not have dreamed up some imaginary postern-gate in Jerusalem called 'the Needle's Eye'. Out of the same dominical mould comes that other word of Jesus about camels, which criticises the misplaced fastidiousness of the Pharisees: 'You blind guides, straining out a gnat and swallowing a camel!' (Matt. 23.24). Hyperbole too is of the dramatic essence of the parable of the Unforgiving Servant (Matt. 18.23-25) whose debt to his master 'ran into millions' and who refused to forgive his fellow-slave who owed him 'a few pounds': as it also lies at the heart of Jesus' warning against censoriousness in the parable of the Splinter and the Plank (Matt. 7.3-5; Luke 6.41f.). Just try to imagine a man with a plank in his eye! Picturesque too in its hyperbole is his word to the disciples about fearlessness in which he tells them that no bird perishes without God, how much less a man! 'The very hairs of your head are all numbered' (Matt. 10.30; Luke 12.7).

Finally, consider his saying about mountain-moving faith (Matt. 17.20, echoed in 1 Cor. 13.2): 'If you have faith as a grain of mustard seed, you will say to this mountain, Move hence to yonder place, and it will move.' Real faith in God, however small, takes seeming impossibilities in its stride. Jesus, as T. W. Manson[1] put it, 'is not inviting Christians to become conjurers and magicians, but heroes like those whose exploits are celebrated in the eleventh chapter of Hebrews.'

Mēden agan 'nothing in excess' was the maxim of the Greeks. No doubt it is an excellent recipe for keeping out of trouble. But the great teachers and writers of mankind have had no such prudential scruples, and the hyperboles of Jesus—his unforgettable exaggerations of nothing less than truth—have meant more to men than all the moralists' cautious counsels of moderation.

[1] *The Sayings of Jesus,* 141.

27. Swearing Peter

(Acts 8.20)

One of the best proofs of the trustworthiness of Mark's Gospel is that 'he does not spare the Twelve', Peter least of all. Mark 'paints him warts and all'. He never seeks to gloss over the fact that this prince among the apostles once sank so low as to disclaim all connexion with his Master —and did it with an oath.

While Jesus was being cross-questioned after his arrest, in the High Priest's house, down below in the 'porch' the bystanders openly taxed Peter with being a follower of the man from Nazareth, now standing before Caiaphas. At this Peter 'broke out into curses and with an oath said, "I do not know this man you speak of" ' (Mark 14.71 NEB). (The Greek verbs are *anathematizein* and *omnuein.*) In other words, Peter called down God's curse on his own head if he were lying and passionately denied all knowledge of the man. (His 'oath' was of course in clear violation of his Master's 'swear not at all' Matt. 5.34ff.) Nowadays Peter would have said, 'May I be damned if, etc.'

Years later there was to be another occasion, in Samaria (Acts 8.20), when Peter gave vent to a curse. According to the AV, when Simon the sorcerer thought to buy the *charisma* of the Holy Spirit from the apostles, Peter replied. 'Thy money perish with thee!' But the operative Greek word in Peter's curse *apōleia*, has, like our 'perdition' (loss of happiness in a future state), eschatological overtones; and the modern English of it, as J. B. Phillips has rightly said, would be, 'To hell with you and your money!'

Needless to say, in all this we are not providing scriptural warrant for using 'bad language'. The Lord's ruling, not Peter's bad example, is mandatory for Christians.

28. Every Christian a Saint

(Acts 9.32)

Some years ago I was introduced to a lady called Mrs. Christian. Intrigued by her married name, I asked her what her maiden one had been. Imagine my surprise when she answered 'Miss Saint'!

All unwittingly she had illustrated a New Testament truth too often forgotten. Every Christian is a saint! If somebody should demur that not a few Christians known to him are more like sinners than saints, the statement is still true. For the Greek word *hagios* 'holy', usually translated 'saint' (from the Latin *sanctus* 'holy') in our New Testament versions, does not describe a paragon of moral perfection; it means someone 'dedicated' to God in Christ—a forgiven sinner, now numbered among God's people and called to live according to his will.

When Peter, for example, went down to visit 'the saints which were at Lydda' (Acts 9.32 AV) he did not expect to find a coterie of what we might call 'super' Christians. The 'saints' at Lydda were the members of the local congregation of God's people; and many of them, we may be sure, were in little danger of being 'canonised'—if there had been such a thing as canonisation in those days. Yet each of them was, in the New Testament sense of the word, a 'saint'. And so is each and everyone today who is a member of Christ's Church, however sorry a specimen of sainthood he may appear to be.

All this 'saintly' confusion arises from the fact that down the centuries the word 'saint' has 'suffered a sea change', has become specialised and rarified, has come to denote not an ordinary, everyday Christian but someone who has, so to speak, passed with high honours in the spiritual life, and is fit for beatification—the first step to canonisation.

But, in order to clarify the difference between those whom the New Testament calls 'saints' and men like, say, Saint Francis, we have got to go back beyond the New Testament to the Old. In the Old Testament one of the names for Israel as God's chosen people was 'the saints of the Most High'. The holiness of these Old Testament saints, however, did not consist in their moral perfection but in the fact that they had been called by God. This was their vocation, a vocation which they might, or might not, live up to. In fact, we know that they often did not.

When Old Israel failed to be the people God meant them to be and rejected Jesus their Messiah, the new Israel—the Church of Christ—served itself heir to the titles and tasks of old Israel. They became known as *hoi hagioi,* the 'dedicated ones', that is, the men and women called by God in Christ to belong to his new people and set apart for his service. That many of them were not 'saints' in our modern sense of the word the New Testament makes very plain. Indeed Paul tells us (1 Cor. 6.11) that many had been, before their conversion, as bad as they could be; and even after their conversion they often showed few signs of qualifying for haloes. Yet in Christ, who had died for their sins, they knew themselves 'justified' (or forgiven) by God. They were, potentially at least, new men and women, and their ultimate destiny was to 'be shaped to the likeness of God's Son' (Rom. 8.29 NEB).

Hoi hagioi, 'the saints' as a title for Christians, occurs some sixty times in the New Testament. No doubt it was because they remembered the Biblical meaning of 'saint' and the change that had come over the word down the centuries, that the NEB translators decided to render the Greek phrase by 'God's people'. The new rendering underscores the fact that every Christian is a saint. It expresses what we might call the sainthood of all believers. It reminds us that we are—even the best of us—'justified sinners'. But if it democratises the idea of sainthood, it should not permit us to forget that our calling is even higher than that of old Israel. Under the Old Covenant God's command to his people had been, 'You shall be holy, for I the Lord your God am holy'

(Lev. 19.2).   The New Testament, by the lips of Christ himself, pitches the demand still higher, 'You shall be all goodness, as your heavenly Father is all good' (Matt. 5.48 NEB).   And that is calling high enough for any saint—ancient or modern.

29. What the Dabbler said

(Acts 17.18)

When the Stoic and Epicurean philosophers of Athens flung the epithet *spermologos* at Paul, what nuance of disdain did they seek to convey?

Starting from a literal meaning of 'seed-pecker'—the bird which picks up scraps in the gutter—the word came to mean a lounger who, magpie-like, collects odds and ends in the market-place.   Four hundred years before, in Athens, Demosthenes had applied this abuse-word to his great rival Aeschines.   Perhaps it was a piece of Athenian slang which carried the suggestion of plagiarism rather than of mere loquacity.

Let us look at what our translators have made of it.   AV, RV and RSV are content with 'babbler' suggesting senseless volubility.   Moffatt paraphrases it as 'this fellow with his scraps of learning', which reminds us of Browning's *Karshish*. The Jerusalem Bible plumps for 'parrot'.   'Charlatan' is the NEB's preference, combining the two ideas of chattering and pretence.   ('Charlatan'—a word we stole from the French who had adopted it from the Italian *ciarlare* 'chatter' —now means a mere talking pretender, but was originally a man who talked fast to sell his wares, so incurring men's suspicion of his honesty.)   But perhaps best of all is Ronald Knox's 'dabbler'.   'Dabble' is what the grammarians call the frequentative of 'dab', the action of a bird, as 'dabbling' conveys the motion of sciolism—superficial pretension to knowledge.   Paul, it seemed to the Athenian philosophers and *flaneurs* who, as Dr. Luke tells us in 'the most Attic remark in the New Testament', 'had no time for anything but talking or hearing about the latest novelty' (NEB), was, like some modern religious cranks, a 'dabbler' in all sorts of bizarre divinities.

Well, eventually they had him before the august Court of the Areopagus who met in the Royal Portico. What did the 'dabbler' say to them in his Areopagitica?

'Two things strike me in it,' said 'Rabbi Duncan[1]: 'His considerable tact in recognising all good he found in Athens; and how he laid the axe to the root of the tree of Attic pride.' Paul did not begin by denouncing them as godless pagans: he began by calling them 'rather religious' (*deisidaimonesterous*), and went on, later, to quote from their own poets. But he did not pretend that their 'religiosity' had got them anywhere. 'The very altars and images which I saw as I strolled round your city' he said, 'confess your ignorance of God. I will tell you agnostics who he really is.' That was a very bold thing to say—to them.

In the sermon which followed—which we take to be Luke's own summary of what Paul said—Paul made three points.

First he said, 'Your thought of God is far too small. God is the universal Creator and Life-giver. You may pride yourselves on being autochthons—men sprung from the native soil of Attica—and call the rest of men "barbarians". I tell you, all mankind is one in God who created them so, so that you have no reason for pride in your racial superiority.'

Next he said, 'This true God shapes the destiny of men and nations. He has given them the whole earth to live in and has providentially appointed seasons for them, hoping that they would seek after and find him. No remote and inaccessible Deity, he is very near to us all, as your own poets have said: "in him we live and move and exist": we are in fact his children made in his likeness. An end, therefore, to all man-made images of him.'

Finally he said: 'God has now resolved on a new start for mankind. Overlooking your past ignorance, he is now calling on you to "repent"—to turn anew to him. For God the

[1] *Colloquia Peripatetica*, 20.

Creator is also the Lord of history which is moving on towards Judgment Day. On that day his agent will be a man of his own choosing (Was Paul thinking of Dan. 7.13 and Jesus' title of the Son of Man?); and as proof that this is so, God has raised this man from the dead.'

Paul's 'Areopagitica', as we call it, was not the whole Gospel of God's grace to sinners in Christ: it was but prolegomena to it—a first lesson in Christianity for cultured pagans. How did they take it? Very much as 'cultured pagans' take it today. Some mocked at the very idea of 'resurrection', holding with their modern counterparts that 'Dead men rise up never'. But others, wistfully hoping that there might be something in what the 'dabbler' said, expressed a wish to hear him again. There are still very many like them in our modern world.

30. 'A Bay with a Beach'

(Acts 27.39)

If you are ever lucky enough to holiday on Malta, 'the George Cross Island', your itinerary ought to include a visit to the 'bay with a beach' (though it has now no sand) in the north-west corner of the island where, on an October day in the year A.D. 59. Paul and his shipmates were wrecked after one of the wildest voyages in history. For sheer dramatic power, as well as for its light on the seamanship of the day, there is nothing quite like this 27th chapter of Acts. Nelson is said to have read it in his flagship before Trafalgar, and it is sometimes named 'the sailors' chapter'.

The man, however, who really put it on the map for modern readers was an English yachtsman called James Smith of Jordanhill who in 1848 published *The Voyage and Shipwreck of St. Paul*. Himself an expert sailor in Mediterranean seas, and no mean scholar, he set out to establish, at first hand, the truth of this chapter. Not only did he prove that what tradition had called 'St. Paul's Bay' was in fact the place where the Alexandrian grain ship carrying Paul to Rome was wrecked at 'a place where two seas meet'; but he showed that the whole narrative must have been written by one who was an eye-witness, if not himself a seaman. That man was of course 'dear doctor' Luke, for this chapter belongs to the last of the 'We passages' in Acts where the author is clearly using extracts from his own travel diary.[1]

If any student of the New Testament has an hour to spare for study, he may relive again, in spirit, this most thrilling of all Luke's travel tales. All he needs is a 'first century' map of the Mediterranean, a good modern commentary on Acts, and of course the New Testament in a modern translation. (Here the NEB is at its brilliant best.[2] We are told that when Professor Dodd and his men were translating it, they took counsel of their classical colleagues in order to ensure that all the details of rigging and route, of wind and water, were correct. The result is a chapter as full of nautical jargon as a Captain Hornblower story.)

The voyage began on a coasting vessel from Caesarea on the sea-board of Palestine, with Paul and some other prisoners under the charge of a kindly centurion called Julius. But it was only after they had changed ships at Myra (on the coast of Lycia in Asia Minor) and, embarking on the Alexandrian grain ship, had sailed 'under the lee of Crete' to Fair Havens, that the high drama began. Because the approach of winter had made sailing very dangerous to ships and men, Paul counselled his captors to winter there. But the captain and the ship-owner decided to sail on to Phoenix (Phineka), hoping to find safer harbourage. A soft, south wind encouraged them, but they had not gone far when 'a fierce " North Easter" tore down on the ship' from the Cretan hills, and there was nothing for it but to 'give way and run before it'. Before long, concerned for the ship's timbers they were 'frapping' them with under-trussing cables, and, fearing lest they might be driven on the dreaded 'shallows of

[1] The 'We Sections' are to be found in Acts 16.10-18; 20.5-21.18; 27 and 28.

[2] The quotations that follow are from it.

Syrtis' off Cyrenaica, 'they lowered the mainsail and let her drive'. The next two days, while the tempest continued, found them 'lightening the ship' and 'jettisoning her gear'. Then 'for days on end there was no sign of either sun or stars, a great storm was raging, and our last hopes (says Dr. Luke) of coming through alive began to fade'.

In all this one man, the prisoner Paul, stood calm and unruffled. The ship would be lost, he told them, but he had received a divine assurance that all aboard her would survive. Then, one night, after a fortnight's 'drifting in the Sea of Adria' (the central Mediterranean) two soundings by the sailors convinced them that land was near. So they 'dropped four anchors from the stern (to act as a brake) and prayed for daylight'. At this juncture the sailors tried to lower a boat and escape, 'pretending that they were going to lay out anchors from the bows'. A word from Paul to the centurion stopped this manoeuvre: 'the soldiers cut the ropes of the boat and let her drop away'. 'Shortly before daybreak Paul urged them all to take some food', himself breaking bread before them all after saying a grace. At this the rest 'plucked up courage, took food,' and began to 'lighten the ship by dumping the corn in the sea'.

And so to the climax of Luke's story. When day broke on the fifteenth day, there before them was land and 'a bay with a beach'. So 'they slipped the anchors and let them go, loosened the lashings of the steering-paddles, set the foresail to the wind and let her drive to the beach'. Alas, they found themselves on a spit of land where two seas met, the ship ran aground, its bow sticking fast in the mud, 'while the stern was being pounded to pieces by the breakers'. It was then that the centurion foiled the soldiers' plan to kill the prisoners and so prevent them escaping. Instead he gave orders that the swimmers aboard should make their own way to land, while the non-swimmers should follow 'some on planks, some on parts of the ship'.

We could wish that Luke had told us how Paul came ashore. He had been thrice shipwrecked before this (2 Cor. 11.25). Was he among the swimmers, or did he come ashore in some less dignified way? Eventually, at any rate, all found themselves, by God's providence, safe and sound on an island which they soon identified as Malta. Appropriately enough, Malta (or Melita) is a Phoenician word meaning 'Escape'.

Here then is a true story to stir the pulses of all who are interested in 'those who go down to sea in ships and do business in great waters'. But it is more. It is the record of the intrepid faith of the little Jewish prisoner on his way to Rome to bear testimony to his Lord before Caesar. At every crisis in that unforgettable voyage it is Paul who dominates the scene and puts heart of courage into the ship's company. So in the great emergencies of history a true man of God can often bring timely help when the practical men are at their wits' end. As Isaiah said, 'he who really puts his faith in God shall never be rattled' (28.16).[1]

31. Jesus Christ our Lord

(Romans 1.4)

Familiar words indeed! With the preposition 'through' prefixed to them they have become a liturgical *cliché*. Nowadays we use them quite indiscriminately. Whether we say 'Jesus' or 'Christ' or 'our Lord' we mean the same thing —or rather, the same person. But in the beginning it was not so; each name had its own individual meaning; and it is worthwhile to go back for a moment and try to recover the meaning which each had on the lips of those who used it first.

I

Begin then with the name 'Jesus'. Around the two syllables of that name have gathered some of our most sacred religious associations:

[1] This is how my colleague, the late Professor A. C. Kennedy, used to translate the verse. The New English Bible reads: 'He who has faith shall not waver'.

'Through him the first fond prayers are said
   Our lips of childhood frame';

and, as at the beginning of life, so it is at its ending:

'The last low whispers of our dead
   Are burdened with his name.'

Of all names, none is more precious to Christian ears than the name Jesus; and it is this simple name, without titular addition, which keeps sounding so hauntingly through our greatest hymns from the mediaeval *Dies Irae:*

'Think, good Jesus, my salvation
   Caused thy wondrous Incarnation'

to John Newton's

'How sweet the name of Jesus sounds
   In a believer's ear.'

Yet this name, so single, so preciously holy now, once was so common that Josephus the Jewish historian (A.D. 37-100) mentions twenty men bearing it.[1]

'Jesus' transcribes the Greek *Iesous* which in turn represents the Hebrew Joshua (which means 'Jehovah saves'). Moreover, the New Testament mentions three and probably four other persons who bore this name. In St. Luke's list of our Lord's ancestors stands 'Er the son of Jesus'. In Acts 13.8 we read of the sorcerer Elymas (whom Paul called 'an imposter and a charlatan') whose patronymic was 'Bar-Jesus'. One of Paul's colleagues when he wrote to the Colossians (Col. 4.11) was 'Jesus called Justus'. But there is probably a fourth example. Turn up the NEB at Matt. 27.17 and you will find Pilate saying, 'Which would you like me to release to you—Jesus Bar-abbas, or Jesus called Messiah?'

It comes to us as something of a shock to learn that the same name should be borne by a common cut-throat and by the Saviour himself. (No doubt this is why many scribes suppressed it in Matt. 27.17). But it serves to make our first point, which is that the name 'Jesus'—now for most

[1] It is quite common in Spain and Latin America today.

Christians one of incomparable holiness, so that we shudder when we hear it used profanely—was once as common as John and James are among us today. And does not its very common-ness serve to make more real to us the human life which Jesus once lived on earth?

II

Consider the next name 'Christ'. Today we use it as a personal name, and make it interchangeable with 'Jesus'. But in the beginning it was an official title. 'Christ', the Greek *Christos,* translates the Hebrew *Mashiach,* the Lord's 'Anointed One', the Messiah—that is, the one who, for the Jews, was to be the bearer of God's rule and salvation in the good time coming when God visited and redeemed his people, and the promises made of old through the prophets would all come true. As indeed they did in Jesus, though in living them out he 'crucified' them, becoming the hoped-for deliverer not by the decree of omnipotence but by the 'scandal' of a Cross.

It was upon this—that Jesus is the Messiah—that the first preachers of the Gospel, who were Jews, laid all the stress. 'Every day', we read (Acts 5.42) 'they went steadily on with their teaching in the temple and in private houses, telling the good news of Jesus the Messiah.' (NEB).

But if we read the record in Acts carefully, we shall see that the apostles changed their language as they changed their audience. To the philosophers of Athens Paul preached not Jesus the Messiah but 'Jesus and the Resurrection' (Acts 17.18). And at Antioch, the cradle of Gentile Christianity, 'men from Cyprus and Cyrene spoke to the Greeks, preaching the *Lord* Jesus.' (Acts 11.20).

III

This verse appropriately brings us to the last of the three titles—the name 'Lord', in Greek *Kyrios,* which was added to interpret the name Christ' for Gentile ears.

The message of the first preachers, whose audiences were mostly Jewish, had been 'Jesus is the Messiah'. But as

Christianity moved out into the wider world which had no Old Testament in its hands, and for whom the word 'Messiah' would have meant as little as the word *Mahdi* means to English ears today, the earlier creed took another form, 'Jesus is Lord' (1 Cor. 12.3, Phil. 2.11).

Now in the first century A.D. 'Lord' was a divine title intelligible to the whole Eastern world; and to call Jesus 'Lord' was to acknowledge his essential divinity.

So Paul can write to the Romans, 'If thou shalt confess Jesus as Lord and shalt believe in thy heart that God raised him from the dead, thou shalt be saved' (Rom. 10.9). And to the Corinthians, 'For although there may be many so-called gods in heaven or on earth . . . yet for us there is one God the Father . . . and one Lord Jesus Christ.' (1 Cor. 8.5f.).

'For us there is one Lord, Jesus Christ.' This is the faith of all the New Testament writers. For none of the earliest Christians was Jesus simply one in a row of religious teachers. Paul, Apollos, Cephas—they were together, here. Jesus, there, apart in a place which none shared or could share— this was how they saw it. Not 'Jesus the man for others' as the 'honest to God' theologians would have us re-write our Christology and make it acceptable to modern man, but 'Jesus the Lord' is the distinctive New Testament faith.

IV

One word still remains to be noticed, the word 'our'. It is not 'Jesus Christ the Lord' but 'Jesus Christ our Lord.' And with that little word 'our' what without it would be merely Christian doctrine becomes personal religion.

What is it to be a Christian? Few questions have evoked such diverse answers. For myself, I know none so simple or sufficient as this: to be a Christian is to call Jesus Lord. It is to put him on the throne of our life and to make him the master-light of all our spiritual seeing.

80

32. Face-lifting

(Romans 2.11)

Reading the divines of a former generation you may come across, as I did recently, the curious word ' prosopolepsy.' It sounds, on first hearing, like a distant cousin of 'epilepsy'. In fact, it is a moral and spiritual disease which is still much prevalent among men and to which, the Bible says, God is immune.

'Prosopolepsy' is the Greek word *prosopolēpsia* (or *prosopolēmpsia*) in English dress. A compound of two Greek words, *prosōpon* 'face' or 'mask' and *lambanein* 'receive', it goes back to the Hebrew Old Testament. There *panīm nāsā* means 'lift the face'. The men who turned the Old Testament into Greek rendered the phrase by combining *prosōpon* and *lambanein*. For us 'face-lifting' is a surgical operation to smooth out and improve one's features. For the men of the Bible it meant 'respect of persons', 'partiality', 'favour-itism'.

The phrase suggests the Oriental mode of greeting. When you met a man—especially a superior—you modestly bowed your face earthwards. If he was disposed to recognise you and show you goodwill, he 'lifted up your face'—accepted you. Inevitably the phrase tended to acquire a pejorative meaning (as it always has in the New Testament). To 'lift up the face' meant to defer to a man unfairly, to show him undue favour. It might happen, for instance, in a law-court when the prospect of a fat bribe might sway a judge's verdict. So judges in the Old Testament are solemnly warned, 'You shall not lift up faces', i.e. 'You shall not be partial' (Deut. 1.17, 16.19). As God the Judge of all, who does not look on outward appearances but on the heart (1 Sam. 16.7), does not 'lift up faces', so earthly judges should seek to be like him (Deut. 10.17).

In the New Testament you find this idiom carried over into the speech of the apostles. Sometimes they talk about 'receiving' (or 'looking on') a man's face, and four times they use the noun 'prosopolepsy'.

In Paul's famous *exposé* of 'the sin of man' (Rom. 1.18-3.20) where he shows that all men, Gentiles and Jews, are sinners alike in God's sight, he tells the Jews, 'There is no face-lifting—no partiality—with God' (Rom. 2.11.). In modern terms, there is no 'most favoured nation clause' in God's dealings with men. (This to the Jews who supposed that because they were the chosen people, they might, as *rentiers* on God's favour, expect preferential treatment on Judgment Day.)

So in Acts 10, after Peter had seen the vision of 'a thing that looked like a sheet of sail-cloth' with creatures in it of every sort, and heard a heavenly voice reproving him for discriminating between 'clean and unclean', he confessed to Cornelius and his friends at Caesarea, 'I now see how true it is that God has no favourites' (Acts 10.34 NEB). Put otherwise, it is clearly God's will that all men, Gentiles no less than Jews, should share in the salvation which he is offering in Christ.

Turn now to Eph. 6.9, and you find Paul reminding masters of households that, as their Master in heaven 'has no favourites', no more should they have. And in Col. 3.25, this time addressing servants, he reiterates the impartiality of the Lord in dealing with sinners.

What Peter and Paul say, James says also. There must be no 'face-lifting'—no favouritism—in the Christian Church, for example, by fawning on the rich and despising the poor. Such favouritism is sin (Jas. 2.1-9).

'God has no favourites' is what the apostles say with one voice. Of course, even to them this was no new doctrine—it was writ large in the Old Testament—in Deuteronomy and elsewhere, and perhaps most wonderfully of all in the book of Jonah. But it is one of these doctrines to which sinful men, blinded by racialism and bigotry, are prone to turn deaf ears, so that even to Peter it came as 'a revolutionary revelation'.

It is a revelation that is still needed—as we need modern prophets like Trevor Huddleston to preach it. The plain

82

uncomfortable fact, it has been said, is that we still should like God to have favourites, provided we were the favoured ones. But the plain uncomfortable fact is also that, whether we like it or not, God still remains no respecter of persons.

In our world 'prosopolepsy' raises its ugly head in many forms and many countries—in the pernicious South African doctrine of *apartheid,* for example, as well as in other nations professing to be Christian who, by their attitudes, would seem to regard God as the Father of the white men only. So far as Christians are concerned, the only cure for it would seem to be a constant preaching of a true doctrine of God, a God who has no favourites. That, and a resolute determination by us Christians, in our daily practice, to treat all men as equals in the sight of the All-Father.

33. *Hoi Polloi*

(*Romans 5.18f.*)

Abraham Lincoln once said that God must love the common people because he made so many of them. But men's language, down the centuries, has not shared the divine view of the demos, the people. Does not *hoi polloi*, the Greek for 'the many', mean nowadays the common herd, the rabble? And have not superior university men with honours sometimes nicknamed their brethren with pass degrees the *hoi polloi*?

When a Greek referred to 'the many', he meant the greater number, the majority. He thought exclusively, meaning 'many, but not all'. This is English idiom also, well illustrated in the words with which the old Highland minister (Macgregor of Inverallochy) used to preface his marriage service: 'My friends, marriage is a curse to the many, a blessing to the few,—and a great uncertainty to all. Do you venture?'

By contrast, when a Jew used the corresponding Hebrew phrase (*harrabim*), he thought inclusively: he meant 'all', the whole lot.

Now this little piece of knowledge is important for our understanding of the New Testament. All the New Testament writers were Jews (with the exception of Luke), and their Greek words therefore often come to us stained with Hebrew idiom. In other words, by *hoi polloi* they commonly mean 'all' and not 'many, but not all'.

This inclusive meaning comes out very clearly in Rom. 5.19: 'For as by one man's disobedience (Adam's) the many *hoi polloi)* were made sinners, so by one man's obedience (Christ's) the many *(hoi polloi)* will be made righteous'. A glance at the preceding verse will show that by 'the many' Paul means 'all' or, as we might say, 'mankind': 'as one man's trespass led to condemnation for all men, so one man's act of righteousness leads to acquittal and life for all men'.

Now what we have been saying about *hoi polloi* is true also where there is no preceding definite article, no *hoi,* no 'the'. This has important bearing on two famous texts. When we read in Matt. 22.14, 'Many are called, but few are chosen', the meaning is that God invites all men into his Kingdom. It is not a declaration that he invites merely a majority. Even more significant is Mark 10.45 where Jesus says that as the Son of Man he has come to 'give his life a ransom for many'. He means that he is sacrificing himself 'for all', for the common salvation. (Compare 1 Tim. 2.6 which echoes Mark 10.45: 'Jesus who gave himself a ransom for all'.) Does not this give the lie to all suggestions that Christ died merely for 'the elect'?

34. The Logic of Redemption

(Romans 8.32)

Of all the letters ever written it may fairly be claimed that, judged by its influence, Paul's to the Romans is the greatest. Martin Luther called it 'the chief book of the New Testament and the purest Gospel'. To the massive mind of

Coleridge it was 'the most profound work ever written'.

What is there in the letter to warrant these remarkable verdicts? Quite simply, in Romans we have the answer to the question, What is Christianity? by the most original mind in the early Church. And it is a striking fact that, whenever there has been a great revival in Christian life and thought, it has generally been associated with the rediscovery by some-one—an Augustine, a Luther, a Wesley, a Barth—of 'the fifth Gospel'—the Gospel according to Paul as we find it in Romans. Written nineteen hundred years ago, probably in a back street of Corinth, its message still has power to move men to repentance and faith. For in the Gospel of what Paul calls 'the righteousness of God'—'God's way of righting wrong', as the NEB translates it (Rom. 1.17)—is the one convincing proof that God has not left man to stew in the juice of his own sin and wickedness but has acted, once for all, for his rescue in Christ his Son.

Every great book has its supreme passages: and, by common consent, this letter reaches its highest moment in the wonderful eighth chapter, the chapter which begins, as a wise old Scots woman once put it, with 'no condemnation' and ends with 'no separation'.

Now in the tremendous climax which rounds off this chapter there is one short verse—the thirty-second—which seems to contain in itself the whole logic of redemption—its premiss and its conclusion.

'He did not spare his own Son but gave him up for us all'—that is the premiss; and at once we are reminded that every-thing in the Gospel goes back to the self-sacrifice of God.

Some people will tell you that the message of Christianity can be summed up as 'God is love'. But a vague reliance on the love of God, even as manifested by Christ, is not Christian faith, nor can a general trust in a heavenly Father's kindness match the deepest need of man or measure up to the world's crises and calamities. No, the heart of the Gospel is not 'God is love' but 'God loved the world so much that he gave . . . '. The Gospel is not an idea, however sublime, but the good news of an act—an act of God in the very stuff of our human history, God's giving of his Son to death to deal, once and for all, with the wrongest thing in the world which is sin. 'He who did not spare his own Son', is Paul's way of putting it; and straightway we are reminded, as we need to be reminded, that, when Christ died on Calvary, God was not only there but was suffering too.

The Cross, then, is the revelation of the suffering love of God, as Abelard insisted. In Helen Waddell's historical novel about the great mediaeval theologian, Abelard and his friend Thibault find a little rabbit crushed in a trap. Abelard breaks out to his friend, 'Do you think there's a God at all?' 'I know, I know,' replies Thibault, 'only I think God is in it too.' 'In it?' Do you mean it makes him suffer? You mean Calvary?' 'Yes, but that was only a piece of it—the piece we saw—in time. Like that.' Thibault pointed to a fallen tree, sawn through the middle. 'That dark ring there, it goes up and down the whole tree. But you only see where it is cut across.'

A moving illustration? Yes, but there is a yet profounder reading of the Cross than Abelard's. It is that which you find in Paul—and in his great modern successor, P. T. Forsyth. In his book *The Justification of God* Forsyth insists that there is no 'theodicy'—no justification of God and his ways with men in the world and history, except in a theology of the Cross; and that not merely as a revelation but as an eternal act of redemption, which gives us the key to his whole dealings with men, and the goal he has in view for his world.

What, he asks, is the ultimate purpose and meaning of all the sins and sufferings of men down countless centuries? Ask your philosophers, and they cannot answer. There is no answer in terms of pure reason; but there *is* one in terms of the Christian Gospel of redemption. God's answer is in his act—in Christ and his Cross, and in that act God is saying to us: 'The misery of man down the ages—do you stumble at the cost? It has cost me more than you. For it cost me my only and beloved Son to justify my name of righteousness and to realise the destiny of my creature in holy love. . . . I am no spectator of the course of things. I spared not my own Son. We carried the load that crushes you. It bowed him into the ground. On the third day he rose with a new creation in his hand, and a regenerate world, and all things working together for good to love and the holy purpose in love. And what he did I did. How I did it? How I do it? This you know not now, and could not, but you shall know hereafter. There are things the Father must keep in his own hand. Be still and know that I am God, whose mercy is as his majesty, and his omnipotence is chiefly in forgiving, and redeeming, and settling all souls in worship in the temple of a new heaven and a new earth full of holiness. In that day the anguish will be forgotten for joy that a New Humanity is born into the world.'[1]

This, and no other, is the God of the Christian Gospel; and when Christian faith rises to the height of this God, it can cry, 'The world is his, whether in maelstrom or volcano, whether it sinks to Beelzebub's grossness or rises to Lucifer's pride and culture. The thing is done, it is not to do.[2]

All this is implicit in Paul's premiss. Now look at the conclusion which he draws. 'He who did not spare his own Son but gave him up for us all,' he says, 'will he not also give us all things with him?'

The finest comment here is Denney's.[3] 'The Christian faith in Providence', he says, 'is an inference from Redemption. The same God who did not spare his only Son will freely give us all things.' In other words, it is because of the Cross that we Christians may be sure of the daily providence of God. Because God has done the first and supreme thing,—given his Son—we may be sure he will guide us and give us all we need. From the fact of redemption we are to be sure of daily providence.

But 'providence'! What a cold and bloodless word it is! You never find Christ using long, abstract words like this. He does not say (with the old Scots proverb):

> Confide ye aye in Providence,
> For Providence is kind.

No, he says, 'Your heavenly Father knows that you have need of all these things. God feeds the wild birds. Will he not much

[1] *The Justification of God*, 164f.
[2] *The Justification of God*, 166.
[3] *Expositor's Greek Testament*, Vol. II, 652.

more feed you? If you, bad as you are, know how to give good gifts to your children, how much more will your heavenly Father give good things to thost who ask him!' (Matt. 6.26, 30; 7.11).

This is the doctrine of providence as a child can understand it. It is not, observe, the doctrine that God will pamper and spoil his children by sparing us all trials and sorrows. These things God will use to discipline and train us for higher service. But it is the assurance that, come weal or woe, God will be with those who love him and that he 'will make all things work together for their good' (Rom. 8.28).

There is one question still unanswered. What does Paul mean by saying that God will give us 'all things'? Here surely we are entitled to interpret the Apostle by his Lord, and for 'all things' read Christ's word '*good* things'. Not fame or wealth or unclouded happiness. Jesus never made such promises to his followers—'in the world,' he said, 'you will have trouble' (John 16.33). No, but daily light and leading and hope, daily forgiveness and help, power to keep us sane and strong amid the storm and wrack of all things, and, at the last, a place in his Father's house with its many rooms (John 14.2).

Do you believe this? And in that faith will you front the world and the future, and life, and death?

35. *Charisma*

(*Romans 12.6*)

It is common knowledge that Biblical words have a way of passing into everyday speech and being secularised and sometimes profaned. The latest Biblical word to suffer the same fate appears to be *charisma* (Englished as 'charism') now rapidly becoming a jargon word of journalists unaware of its lofty origins and connotations. Thus in his radio obituary of her on Dec. 13, 1968 the BBC's correspondent declared, 'Tallulah Bankhead had glamour, or as we now call it, charisma.' (About her portrayal of Cleopatra on the New York stage some years before an American critic had not been so flattering. 'Miss Bankhead,' he wrote, 'barged up the Nile—and then sank.')

So *charisma* apparently becomes a synonym for glamour which, we are told, nowadays means 'oomph' or 'sex appeal'. To discover how the word has fallen from its high estate let us turn back from the twentieth century to the first.

In the New Testament, where it occurs 17 times, *charisma* is certainly not of the earth, earthy. It is a derivative of that sovereign apostolic word *charis*. *Charis* 'grace' means primarily the free forgiving love of God in Christ to sinners and then the operation of that love in the lives of Christians. *Charisma* 'grace-gift' is a particular actualisation of this grace of God and stands for all those spiritual gifts or endowments which Christians possess in various degrees and forms. In the apostolic letters (Rom. 12, 1 Cor. 12, 1 Peter 4, etc.) we find lists of these *charismata* or 'charisms'. They include everything from prophesying and preaching, teaching and healing, speaking with tongues and the discerning of spirits to such practical things as administration, presiding in church, and visitation of the sick. All are regarded as manifestations of the primary gift, the Holy Spirit, and all are utterly removed from any idea of 'glamour' in its Hollywood sense.

Some day perhaps our lexicographers will trace the steps by which *charisma* came down in the world of words; for it is certain that in its New Testament setting it was a holy—a 'numinous'—word.

'Numinous' at once suggests the name of the great German expert on religion, Rudolf Otto, whose book *The Idea of the Holy* made such an impact on theological thinking half a century ago. Was it perhaps, partly at least, through his influence that *charisma* and 'charismatic' (whether as adjective or noun) became vogue words today?

The essence of religion, Otto said, lies not in knowledge or in good conduct but in awe, e.g. the awesome kind of experience described in Isa. 6.1ff or Ps. 139. And there are men whom, because they seem to belong to that world of wonder and mystery—the world of *numen,* or divinity—and to draw

89

their powers from it, we may call 'charismatics'. Not that they themselves make such claims; rather they are experienced by others as such. The 'charismatic' in fact is one on whom God's Spirit rests in a special way, so that he possesses extraordinary gifts or 'charisms'. These need not be specifically religious, for the *charisma* may find expression in art or poetry or music. (One thinks, for example, of Mozart. Once, talking about his ability to hear his symphonies 'all at once'—simultaneously—he said, 'This is the best gift I have to thank my Divine Master for.') But in the religious sphere the 'charismatic' man *par excellence* is the prophet. He is the man who has the power to hear 'the voice within' and, having heard it, to declare, 'Thus saith the Lord'. Yet even the prophet does not represent the highest stage—a stage of revelation as underivable from that of the prophet as the prophet's is from that of the common man. At this highest stage the Spirit of God indwells the man 'without measure' (John 3.34): in him holiness—the *numen*—is embodied and incarnate. 'Such a man,' Otto said, 'is more than a prophet. He is the Son.'[1]

That Jesus had such a *charisma* the Gospels make clear. The disciples felt this on the Mount of Transfiguration; Peter felt it when he cried, 'Depart from me, for I am a sinful man, O Lord' (Luke 5.8); and it appears, perhaps most wonderfully of all, in Mark 10.32: 'And they were on the road going up to Jerusalem, and Jesus was walking ahead of them; and they were amazed, and those who followed were afraid.'

Nor have the disciples been alone in this feeling about Jesus and his *charisma*. Men have felt thus about him all down the centuries. Perhaps this testimony of Immanuel Kant, little known and unexpected as it is, may stand for many more. Once when an indiscreet admirer mentioned his name in the same breath as Christ's, the great philosopher recoiled in horror. 'The one is holy,' he said, 'the other is that of a poor bungler doing his best to interpret him.'

The *charisma* of Jesus Christ was the very grace and holiness of deity. The *charisma* of Tallulah Bankhead was earthy glamour. This is the measure of the word's 'fall from grace'.

[1] *The Idea of the Holy*, 182.

36. Grace and Peace

(1 Corinthians 1.3 etc.)

In the first century A.D., if you were a pagan, when you wrote to your friend, you wished him *chairein*—a kind of 'cheerio'. If you were a Jew, you wished him *shalōm* 'peace'. If you were a Christian you wished him 'grace and peace from God the Father and the Lord Jesus Christ'. When Paul and the other apostolic writers used this formula, what were they wishing for their readers?

They certainly were not asking God and Christ to make them lithe and lovely or to preserve them from foreign aggressors. Yet loveliness of outward form and freedom from war had been the original meanings of the two Greek words, *charis* and *eirēnē*, which they used.

Basically, *charis* means that which gives pleasure or delight. When Homer and the old Greeks used the word, it meant beauty, charm, attractiveness, whether of person or of movement. From this it was an easy transition to the meaning of 'favour'—favour felt on the part of the doer—kindness—or favour felt on the part of the receiver—gratitude.

But when the Jews and later the Christians took over the word, it acquired new and significant nuances. Its first elevation came when the men who turned the Old Testament into Greek used the word to render the common Old Testament phrase 'find favour (*chēn*) with God'. Its second elevation came when the apostles used it to express the heart of their 'good news', or Gospel, namely, the free favour of God to undeserving men—the kind of quality men had seen incarnate in Jesus during the days of his flesh, that wonderful kindness to sinners, that concern for the last, the least, and the lost, which had been the very soul of his ministry on earth.

So men began to speak of 'the God of all grace' or of 'the grace of the Lord Jesus Christ'; and 'grace' for them meant, in James Denney's classical definition, 'the love of God spontaneous, beautiful, unearned, at work in Jesus Christ for the salvation of men'.

Thus what began as a *shining* word ended up as a *loving* one,—came to express the central truth of the 'Fact of Christ'. In the prologue to his Gospel St. John wrote, 'The law was given through Moses but grace and truth—gracious reality— came through Jesus Christ' (John 1.17). If any man, however, had the right to call himself the preacher of grace, it was the apostle Paul. Eighty-eight times the word occurs in his letters, and often it is a single-word expression for the Gospel. The Gospel he defines as 'the good news of the grace of God' (Acts 20.24). It is by grace, he says, that we have been saved (Eph. 2.5), by grace he himself is what he is (1 Cor. 15.10). Where sin abounded, he says of the good news of the Gospel, grace superabounded (Rom. 5.20), and Christians are 'no longer under law but under grace'—that is, no longer under the rule of statutes but living in the glad sunshine of God's favour (Rom. 6.15).

Grace, then is 'the antecedent being and act of God which is the ground of all Christian experience' (Barrett). 'Peace' the word which Paul and the apostles generally conjoin with 'grace', is the outcome of God's saving act, the total state of well-being to which men are admitted.

But, to explain this, we must take a closer look at the earlier history of the word *eirēnē*.

In classical Greek *eirēnē* had meant mostly freedom from strife or war. But turn to the Old Testament and you find 'peace' (Heb. *shalōm*, Grk. *eirēnē*) being pressed into the service of the one true God. In psalmist and prophet 'peace' denotes the cessation of God's anger with his people. 'Let me hear what God the Lord will speak,' says the Psalmist, 'for he will speak peace to his people' (Ps. 85.8). And the Lord speaking through Isaiah declares, 'I will not contend for ever . . . but my word will be, Peace, peace to the far and to the near' (Isa. 57.19).

If we now pass to the New Testament we find that 'peace' comes to mean the reconciliation between God and men accomplished by God's saving work. Peter says to Cornelius,

'You know the word which God sent to Israel, preaching good news of peace by Jesus Christ' (Acts 10.36). For the apostles 'peace' meant not only the cessation of God's holy displeasure with sinners but also the inner and triumphant serenity which comes to men who have accepted the good news of God's reconciling love in Christ. 'We have peace with God,' Paul says, 'through our Lord Jesus Christ . . . and we rejoice in hope of sharing the glory of God' (Rom. 5.1.). And all climaxes in the statement of Eph. 2.14, 'He is our peace'. Christ (Paul would say) not only brings us a new concept of peace (Cf. John 14.27 'My peace I give to you') he embodies it; he is it.

St. Paul talked both of the 'grace of God' and 'the peace of God'. If by the first he meant the extravagant goodness of God in Christ to sinners, by the second, which follows from it, he did not mean some sort of divine passivity or inertia. 'The peace of God,' said P. T. Forsyth, 'is not a glassy calm but a mighty confidence':

> I steadier step
> when I recall,
> That though I slip,
> Thou dost not fall.

37. The Imitation of Christ

(1 Corinthians 11.1)

The apostles bid us imitate Christ. 'Be imitators of me,' said St. Paul to the Corinthians, 'as I am of Christ (1 Cor. 11.1). St. John urges his readers to 'live as Christ himself lived' (1 John 2.6 NEB). St. Peter says Christ left us an example that we should follow in his steps (1 Peter 2.21). But how do we do it in this 20th century?

All down the Christian centuries men have agreed that the Christian life must be in some way the endeavour to 'catch his great accents' and 'make him our pattern to live and die'. But in what sense? A *literal* imitation of Christ is obviously 'out'. It would mean learning Aramaic, leading the life of a wandering preacher, and severing all those ties and claims which are, for most of us today, the concrete material of Christian living. And even if such an imitation were possible, it would be a dead, mechanical imitation like the production of factory-made models. How then can Christ be 'exemplary' for us today?

Imitation has ever been a potent and legitimate factor in human behaviour and education. Children have imitated parents, students have responded to the tones and temper of a supreme teacher, patriots have rallied to the challenge of a great leader. Ought our imitation of Christ to be of this kind? Does it mean taking Jesus as our spiritual hero and trying to match our manhood to 'the manhood of the Master'?

In the last hundred years many attempts have been made by our scholars to re-tell, with the help of modern knowledge, the story of 'the Jesus of History'. And unconsciously there has arisen the idea that following Christ's example means the *moralistic* imitation by us of the towering moral stature of the man Jesus. So, in much Christian nurture and education, he has been held up as supreme example for imitative moral effort. Faced with our own problems, we have asked, 'What would Jesus have done in such and such a situation?' We have almost made the Christian life consist in a latter-day discipleship to Jesus an admired person in past history.

It comes therefore as a surprise to find how little the first Christians shared this view. They never thought of him merely as a person in past history; they had no wish to turn back the clock and return to the dear, dead days in Galilee. That master-disciple relationship had in fact ended at the Cross. Not once in the letters of the apostolic writers is Christ described as 'Master' (*didaskalos*): not once are Christians called 'disciples'. For them, the paramount miracle is not Jesus as a hero of past history, but Christ the Lord, present now through the Holy Spirit; and following Christ means for them life in a quite new fellowship—the company of those in whom the living Christ moves and works.

94

If a literal imitation of Christ is an impossibility, by New Testament standards the moralistic imitation of Jesus an admired person in past history, is mistaken. What then? In our time the swing of the pendulum seems to have taken us to the opposite extreme. Some of our modern theological mentors assure us that the man Jesus was not, historically regarded, a very remarkable person after all, and that it is foolish and wrong to feed Christian faith and practice by an appeal to the historical Jesus of the Gospel story. Moreover, they tell us that, when the apostles bid us imitate Christ, the qualities to be imitated are not the virtues of a human person but of a divine being. The apostles wish us to copy not the human Jesus but the heavenly Christ.

This view is as one-sided and ultimately as wrong as the 'Moral Hero' one we have rejected. Take first the point about the 'exemplariness' of Christ in the apostolic letters. Paul undoubtedly holds up Christ as our example in such passages as Rom. 15.3, 2 Cor. 8.9 and Phil. 2.6. It is no less true that when he does so, his statements have a Christological character, since he always argues from fellowship with a risen Lord. But for Paul—and this is the heart of the matter—Christ is not just the Jesus of history or the heavenly Christ; he is *both,* in an indissoluble unity. He is the one who was once born of a woman, made under the Law, and nailed to a Cross, who is now the Lord of glory.

The second point is this. The first Christians did not despise the inspiration and guidance to be derived from a knowledge of the pre-Resurrection life of Jesus. On the contrary, they treasured up stories of his deeds and records of his words in that oral tradition which was later written down in our Gospels. These Gospels were written not so much to create faith as to *feed* it, to help men in their Christian living, to enable them, with the Holy Spirit's help, to 'live as Christ lived'.

We come back then to our opening question: In what sense can our Christian life today be an imitation of Christ?

The answer is that, however much the world has changed in nineteen centuries, our imitation of Christ must mean basically what it meant to the saints of Salonika, Corinth, Colossae,

Ephesus and Rome. It cannot be an attempt to return to the master-disciple relationship of Galilee, a moralistic striving to match the manhood of the master. Like the Christians addressed in the New Testament epistles, we stand on the Easter side of the Gospel story; we are post-ascension Christians. We belong to that fellowship created by the Resurrection, empowered by the Pentecostal gift of the Spirit, and now numbering more than nine hundred millions in the earth—of which Christ is the living and regnant Head. By his power at work in us, through the Holy Spirit, we seek to pattern our lives on Christ's—to live, as Paul put it in Col. 2.8, 'according to Christ'. But when we ask what that pattern is to be, we must go back, like the first Christians, to the grace and goodness, the gentleness and love, the obedience and self-sacrifice that shines for us in him who is the central figure in the Gospel story.

Unless we are idiots or blasphemers, we don't say, 'I mean to be as good as Christ was'. In any case, such an attitude would not be Christian, for it would put *me* in the very centre of the picture and make my own sinful and selfish will the prime factor in my regeneration. Growth in character—or as the New Testament would say, growth in grace—does not come this way. Does it not always come by appropriating energies from outside ourselves and yielding ourselves to life-giving influences? So real Christianity begins with God and his grace, not with ourselves. We cannot, by some ethical *tour de force,* make ourselves like Christ, but we can 'be made like him'—as the Spirit of God in Christ does his beneficent work in us and brings forth his 'fruit'—if we are humbly willing to 'learn of Christ', bring our lives to the test of his standards, and yield ourselves to his influence.

38. *Marana-tha*

(1 Corinthians 16.22)

How many readers of the AV must have been mystified by
I Cor. 16.22:

'If any man love not the Lord Jesus Christ, let him be
anathema maran-atha'.

Clearly *anathema* expresses some kind of curse; and the
lack of a full-stop after it suggests that *maran-atha* is an
additional piece of imprecatory mumbo-jumbo.

Anathema, a Greek word, signifies 'something devoted' to
a deity, either for consecration or for cursing. (Our English
word 'blessed'—like the French *sacré*—is similarly ambi-
valent. It can mean 'divinely happy', as in the Beatitudes,
or it can mean 'accursed' as in our colloquial 'I can't find
the blessed thing'.) In Paul's letter it is obviously used in
the bad sense, and 'let him be accursed' is the English of it.

But the second part of Paul's 'curse' is Aramaic, our Lord's
mother-tongue. It begins with the Aramaic *mar* 'Lord' and
it ends with some part of the Aramaic verb for 'come'.
Formerly men took it as indicative, and divided the phrase
thus '*maran-atha*—'Our Lord comes'—making it a confession.
Nowadays, the general opinion is that *tha* is the Aramaic
imperative, and that the division should be *marana-tha* 'Our
Lord, come'. This view seems confirmed, first, by the words
near the end of Revelation 'Come, our Lord' (Rev. 22.20)
and, second, by the occurrence of the Aramaic word at the
close of a prayer in the *Didache*, a church manual probably
compiled in Syria at the end of the first Christian century.
Marana-tha is therefore probably a prayer from the Aramaic-
speaking Mother Church of Jerusalem.

What kind of prayer? We know that the early Christians
expected Christ's 'royal coming', or *Parousia*. We naturally
therefore take it as a petition for Christ to come at the End.

But in the *Didache* it closes the liturgy for the Lord's Supper. 'Where two or three are gathered together in my name', Jesus had said (Matt. 18.20) 'there am I in the midst of them'. Must it not also have been a prayer used by the early Christians at their eucharists when they invoked their living Lord to grace their meal with his presence, as he had done on the first Easter Day (Luke 24.35; Acts 10.41):

> Come, Lord Jesus, and be our Guest,
> And bless what Thou bestowèd hast.

Thus this little piece of Aramaic had a three-fold reference: (1) It looked back to the first Easter Day; (2) it invoked the presence of the risen Lord, through the Spirit, when the early Christians met to 'break bread'; and (3) it called on the Lord to come in glory.

So far from being a piece of imprecatory mumbo-jumbo, *marana-tha* is probably the earliest Christian prayer.

39. *Arrabōn*

(2 Corinthians 1.22, 5.5; Ephesians 1.14)

When I was a little lad and there was a party pending in the manse, I used to slip into the kitchen where my mother was busy baking. There, as a special favour or 'treat', I would be given, straight from the 'girdle' *(Anglicé,* 'griddle') a warm and succulent pancake—as a foretaste, or as the lexicographers define it, 'a part given in advance of what will be freely bestowed afterwards'. This was my first experience of what Paul calls an *arrabōn.*

The word is Semitic in origin and originally meant 'earnest money'. From the Hebrew *ērabōn* we can trace it through the Latin *arra* to the Scots 'arles' (the 'arles penny' was the advance payment you made when you were hiring a servant). Always the basic meaning of the word is a foretaste, a first instalment and pledge that what is to follow will be of the same quality. (In modern Greek *arrabona* is an 'engagement ring'). Turn up the Greek papyrus letters, written about the time of Christ, which our archaeologists have been exhuming from the sands of ancient Egypt, and you will find it used there. Thus a man writes to his friend, 'I paid Lampon the mouse-catcher for you the sum of eight drachmae as earnest-money in order that he may catch the mice while they are with young'.

But an *arrabōn* has not always meant actual money. Two or three centuries ago in Britain the business men who arranged for the sale and transfer of an estate would take the buyer to the property for sale. There they would dig a spadeful of the best soil—or perhaps cull a handful of the finest fruit in the orchard—and give it to him as a pledge of future full possession. And this ceremony, according to the lawyers, gave the purchaser an incontestable right and title to the whole promised property.

Three times in his letters Paul uses this word *arrabōn* of the Holy Spirit. God, he says, has given us the Spirit in our hearts as a pledge and first instalment of what he means to bestow more freely hereafter—of our heavenly inheritance. Our present possession of it is foretaste and guarantee of the life of heaven. For some Christians the mere mention of the Holy Spirit will suggest something 'quite out of this world'. In fact, as the New Testament teaches, the Holy Spirit is the divine dynamic by which, here and now, we are enabled to live the Christian life. It is (in Henry Scougal's phrase) 'the life of God in the soul of men'—a sample in advance of the life of heaven.

Perhaps the finest illustration in Christian history comes from the life of St. Augustine. One evening at Ostia, near Rome, Augustine and his saintly mother Monica were talking about the deep things of God. And, as they conversed, Augustine tells us he was vividly aware that they had left time behind, or got above it. 'Still higher did we climb by the staircase of the Spirit', he says, 'thinking and speaking of Thee and marvelling thy works, O God. And, as we talked and yearned, we touched the life for an instant with the full force of our hearts'.

So deep, so intense was the joy of that experience that Augustine felt that if it could be prolonged, it would be the very life of heaven itself.

Few of us may ever hope to reach these seraphic heights; but surely wherever Christians meet and find themselves in perfect fellowship with one another, there we have 'the fellowship of the Holy Spirit', the fellowship which He creates; there we have an *arrabōn* of the life of heaven.

40. Carnal Christologies

(2 Corinthians 5.16)

'I was arrested (*katelēpthēn*) by Christ Jesus' is Paul's description (Phil. 3.12) of the never-to-be-forgotten experience on the Damascus road which changed the whole trend of his life, and made him 'a man in Christ' (2 Cor. 12.2). But did Paul ever see Jesus 'in the days of his flesh'? We know that he was in Jerusalem, as a pupil of Rabbi Gamaliel, before the crucifixion (Acts 22.3). He tells us that he was back in Jerusalem a few years after it (Gal. 1.18). Was he there in the interval, and did his eyes ever light on the man of Nazareth?

Good scholars have judged it likely. How else (they say) would Paul have been able to recognise Christ on the Damascus road? But were this so, we might have expected Paul to mention the fact quite unequivocally in his letters.

Some have countered by saying that he does just this in 2 Cor. 5.16: 'Though we have known (*egnōkamen*) Christ after the flesh *(kata sarka),* yet now henceforth know we him no more'. But, as modern scholars agree, the AV's translation here is quite misleading. The phrase 'after the flesh', which means 'by what is external' and stands for 'worldly standards', goes not with the noun 'Christ' but with the verb 'we have known', and the reference is to that knowledge of Christ he had *before* his conversion. The RSV brings out

100

Paul's true meaning: 'Even though we once regarded Christ from a human point of view, we regard him thus no longer'. Paul is thinking of the all too human and erroneous picture of Christ he had before he met him on the Damascus road. As 'a Pharisee of the Pharisees' he had thought of Jesus as a messianic Pretender whose crucifixion meant that he had been disowned by God. His conversion brought Paul a quite new understanding of Christ. Now he knew that 'in Christ God was reconciling the world to himself', that God had sent him to save the human race, and that as risen Lord he rightfully claimed the allegiance of all men.

Let us make the same point in another way by considering Gal. 3.13, where Paul says that Christ 'became a curse for us'.) 'Became' is here a circumlocution for the action of God, and 'curse' means 'cursed one'. 'God made Christ a cursed one' is Paul's meaning; he is thinking of Deut. 21.23 'A hanged man is accursed by God'. When you come to consider it, what a truly shocking phrase it is! How and where did it begin? It can only have originated in the time before Paul met the risen Lord. Jesus of Nazareth, a man cursed by God—this was why Paul persecuted him in the person of his followers and 'tried to make them blaspheme' him (Acts 26.11) by saying, 'A curse on Jesus!' (I Cor. 12.3).

After he met the risen Lord Paul still went on saying 'God made Christ a cursed one', only now he added two little words, words that made all the difference, the words 'for us'. From that great day onwards the atoning Cross became 'the diamond pivot', the very heart and centre of his Gospel, and he could go on to expand the terrible paradox of Gal. 3.13 in 2 Cor. 5.21 'For our sake he (God) made him (Christ) to be sin who knew no sin, so that in him we might become the righteousness of God' (or, as the NEB has it, that 'in him we might be made one with the goodness of God himself').

'Knowing Christ after the flesh' therefore means having inadequate, worldly, superficial, one-sided—and therefore wrong—ideas of Christ, ideas that by concentrating on this or that aspect of his life or teaching, or by failing to note the mysterious undercurrent that runs through the whole story of Jesus as told in the Gospels, get their picture of Christ completely out of focus, and are blind to the true secret of his Person. In modern times there have been many such pictures of Jesus. Last century we had Ernest Renan's 'Amiable Carpenter of Galilee', J. R. Seeley's 'Moral Reformer', Leo Tolstoi's 'Spiritual Anarchist'. In this one we have had Klausner's 'Unorthodox Rabbi', Conrad Noel's 'Christ the Revolutionary' and 'the Existentialist Christ' of Rudolf Bultmann. He has been pictured as a great Outlaw, a great Pacifist and a great Socialist. All these pictures of him Paul would have dismissed as portraits according to the flesh, 'carnal christologies'. For him the only true picture would have been that painted on the walls of the catacombs by the early Christians—that picture of a fish, ICHTHUS, whose Greek letters, when they are spelled out, mean 'Jesus Christ, the Son of God, Saviour'.

41. The Preacher's Charter

(2 Corinthians 5.18-20)

What is the true nature of Christian preaching? And how does the preacher differ from the orator, the politician or the propagandist?

There is a true, if irreverent, story about a Scotsman who, after listening to a sermon from his minister (a noted theologian) expressed his sour disapproval to a friend. 'Do you know what he was telling us?' he said. 'That it wasn't really he himself who was preaching, but God. Well, all I can say, God is a very poor preacher.'

If our captious Scotsman had heard St. Paul, he might have had the same complaint. How the apostle conceived of Christian preaching comes out in 2 Cor. 5.18-20:

[18]'All this is from God, who through Christ reconciled us to himself and gave us the ministry of reconciliation; [19]that is, God was in Christ reconciling the world to himself, not

counting their trespasses against them, and entrusting to us the message of reconciliation. [20]So we are ambassadors for Christ, God making his appeal through us. We beseech you on behalf of Christ, be reconciled to God.' (RSV).

Observe that God's work of reconciliation in Christ and the message about it are inseparable, as is shown by the parallel clauses of v.18 ('who through Christ reconciled us to himself, and gave us the ministry of reconciliation') and also by the explanatory v.19 ('God was in Christ reconciling the world to himself . . . and entrusting to us the message of reconciliation'). For Paul, preaching was itself a part of God's saving action. (Incidentally this explains why he can speak in the first verse of the next chapter about 'sharing God's work'.) The point is clinched by his 'We are ambassadors for Christ' (v.20). Paul's preaching derives its authority from the fact that Christ himself speaks in the word of his ambassador, or, what for Paul amounts to the same thing, 'God makes his appeal' to men, using the apostle as his mouthpiece.

A like high concept of preaching—that it is an Act prolonging God's great Act, mediating it, conveying it—appears in Rom. 1.16 where Paul says that the Gospel 'is the power of God unto salvation to everyone who has faith.' Note that he calls the Gospel God's *dunamis*, his 'mighty work', his miracle. Now of course the Gospel is about God's 'mighty work' in Christ incarnate, crucified and risen—it is the proclamation of a dynamic divine event. But here, quite clearly, Paul thinks of the Gospel as being itself a part of that continuing event.

Is Paul alone in holding this high view of preaching? On the contrary, he is supported in it by many great names down the centuries. 'The preaching of the divine Word,' said Johann Bullinger the Swiss Reformer and friend of Calvin, 'is the divine Word.' 'Preaching,' said P. T. Forsyth, 'is the Gospel prolonging and declaring itself'. And he added, 'No true preaching of the Cross can be any other part of the action of the Cross.' J. S. Stewart[1] agrees: 'The proclamation of the Word belongs itself to *Heilsgeschichte* as an integral

[1] *A Faith to Proclaim*, 43.

103

part of God's continuous saving activity.' In short, true Christian preaching is the timeless link between God's great saving Act in Christ and sinful man's apprehension of it. It is the dynamic medium through which God contemporises his historic (and saving) self-disclosure in Christ his Son, and offers men the opportunity of responding in faith (which is a taking of God at his Word in Christ).

The Scottish divine who seemed to his hearer to be setting himself up as some kind of mouthpiece of the All Highest had good warrant for his doctrine. If only we could get this doctrine of preaching accepted, worked out and acted on by our ministers, divinity students and all who do the work of evangelists, what a mighty revolution we might have in the spiritual work of the Church!

42. A Thorn in the Flesh

(2 Corinthians 12.7)

The phrase has passed into popular parlance; but how many who use it have any idea what controversy it has caused down the centuries, how many learned dissertations it has produced!

Let us consider the original context in 2 Cor. 12. After telling his readers of the wonderful revelations and 'raptures' which had befallen him, more than a dozen years earlier, when he 'was caught up into the third heaven' and 'heard words so secret that human lips may not repeat them', Paul declares that, to prevent his being unduly elated by these tremendous experiences, he was given 'a thorn in the flesh', to keep him humble.

Skolops, his Greek word, means 'thorn' or possibly something bigger, a 'stake'. But what was it? In the second century, as Tertullian tells us, it was commonly agreed to have been a severe pain in the head. But in the centuries that followed speculation took many strange turns as one

104

man after another, arguing from his own experience to Paul's, attributed his own 'thorn' to the apostle. 'Not a headache,' said the persecuted fathers of the Church, 'but suffering from his enemies.' 'Concupiscence,' said the monks of the middle ages, feeling carnal longings themselves. 'Spiritual trials and torments,' said Luther, who had himself run the whole gamut of them. And so men have gone on guessing to this very day, and we have had diagnoses from doctors of medicine as well as from doctors of divinity. 'Periodic depressions,' says a modern German psychiatrist. 'It was the heart-break Paul suffered from his failure to persuade his fellow-Jews to accept the Gospel, says a contemporary French theologian.

Amid this gallimaufry of guesses can we reach any certainty about the nature of Paul's 'thorn'?

The only other passage in his letters which sheds light on 2 Cor. 12.7 is Gal. 4.13f. 'It was bodily illness,' Paul tells the Galatians, 'that originally led to my bringing the Gospel to you, and you resisted any temptation to show scorn or disgust ('show disgust' is literally 'spit at') at the state of my poor body; you welcomed me as if I were an angel of God, as you might have welcomed Christ Jesus himself . . . you would have torn out your very eyes and given them to me, had that been possible' (NEB).

Since it is natural to suppose that 2 Cor. 12 and Gal. 4 refer to the same malady, we may infer with some confidence that it was primarily a bodily one. This is the most natural meaning of 'a thorn in the flesh'. 2 Cor. 12 shows that Paul had regarded his 'thorn in the flesh' as a check to his spiritual pride. And Gal. 4 indicates that his malady could not be concealed. Can we take the matter any further?

About 1860 John Brown, M.D., of Edinburgh, the celebrated creator of 'Rab and his Friends', gave his vote for opthalmia. Were not the Galatians ready to give Paul their eyes, if that had been possible? Does not eye trouble explain Paul's 'big letters' in Gal. 6.11? Do we not learn from Dr. Luke that at his conversion Paul had been, temporarily at least, blinded (Acts 9.9)? Yet even each of these three apparently strong arguments can be countered.

Many of the great men in history—Julius Caesar, King

Alfred, Oliver Cromwell, Napoleon, Dostoevsky — have been epileptics. Was Paul's 'thorn' his liability to epileptic fits? This hypothesis has found wide favour in Germany and was espoused by J. B. Lightfoot, the great English scholar. In Paul's day epilepsy was called 'the disease you spat at' (to ward off any evil effects). Is this why Paul says, gratefully, that the Galatians had refused to 'spit at' him? Epilepsy is repulsive to the beholder, as Paul's malady was. It has a way of 'buffeting' the body, as Paul tells us his illness had (2 Cor. 12.7). The disease is intermittent, as Paul's seems to have been. All in all, it sounds a formidable case. Yet it is not conclusive. For (1) pain is not a feature of epileptic fits—and Paul felt acute pain, and (2) recurrent epilepsy causes mental deterioration. What evidence is there that Paul's mind was seriously affected?

We come to the third theory. One of the great scourges in the Asia Minor of Paul's day—a scourge now much mitigated by Sir Ronald Ross's discovery—was malaria. Malarial fever is intermittent. It causes acute pains in the head. 'Like a red-hot bar thrust through the forehead,' says one sufferer; and another, 'a grinding, boring pain in one temple, like the dentist's drill.' 'Like a stake in the flesh,' says the apostle. Further, we know that in Paul's day men regarded malaria as sent by the gods, and when they called down curses on their enemies, wished for them malaria. This, said Sir William Ramsay of Aberdeen, must have been Paul's 'thorn'. Probably he caught malaria in the low coastlands of Asia Minor on the first missionary journey, and took the natural remedy of going inland into the highlands of Galatia.

Ramsay's view undoubtedly makes good sense; yet, in the last analysis, who can say certainly what Paul's 'thorn' was? But if we cannot diagnose Paul's illness, we can learn from him what to do about it.

The thorn, Paul says grimly, was a devil's messenger which dealt him disabling blows. Yet, evil thing as it was, he sees it as a discipline used by God, in his mysterious providence, to make him a better apostle. From his 'thorn' he learned, as we all have to, that the Lord sometimes refuses what we ask in order to give us what we need. 'Three times,' he says, 'I begged the Lord to rid me of it; but his answer was "My grace is all you need; power comes to its full strength in weakness" ' (NEB). Accepting it as the Lord's will for him, Paul came to terms with his affliction, and used it to become 'the happy warrior',

> Who doomed to go in company with pain
> And fear, and bloodshed, miserable train!
> Turned his necessity to glorious gain.[1]

How many soldiers of Christ down the centuries, catching their inspiration from Paul, have turned their crosses into crowns and witnessed gloriously for Christ from the depths of their disablement!

43. The Fortnight's Visit

(Galatians 1.18f)

'Three years later I did go up to Jerusalem to get to know (*historēsai*) Cephas. I stayed with him a fortnight, without seeing any other of the apostles, except James the Lord's brother' (NEB).

Beyond doubt one of the most historic meetings in early Christian history. It brought face to face Christ's two most famous apostles, Peter now much more like 'the Rock' Christ had prophetically nicknamed him, and Paul the erstwhile persecutor now turned preacher of the Christ he had once cursed. Ah, if only we had a tape-recording of their conversations! For we may be very sure that they did not spend all their time discussing the weather.

What was the real purpose of Paul's visit to Jerusalem? And what did Peter and Paul talk about during that fateful fortnight? Our answer turns on the precise meaning we give to the Greek verb italicised above. If Paul had merely wished to 'see' Peter, as the Greeks had wished to 'see' Jesus' (John

[1] Wordsworth, *The Happy Warrior*.

12.21), he must have employed the same ordinary verb as St. John. In fact he used a verb, *historein*, which he never uses elsewhere and which is very rare in Biblical literature.

'Visit' (the usual rendering in our versions)—or 'visit with' as our American friends say—with its implication of the merely social encounter, will hardly do. The root meaning of the verb, as Liddell and Scott say in their lexicon, is to 'visit with the purpose of inquiry'. The NEB's 'get to know' is therefore certainly better than the RSV's 'visit'. Might then this 'visit for the purpose of inquiry' mean, as some have supposed, 'to learn Peter's story'? But 'the Big Fisherman's' story—if by this we mean the story of his first call to be 'a fisher of men', the ups and downs of his discipleship, his confession and rebuke at Caesarea Philippi, the sleeping and the sword-play in Gethsemane, the denial of his Master in the High-priest's courtyard—this, full of human interest as it was, can hardly have been Paul's chief concern. If 'inquiry' is the true nuance of Paul's verb, there is much to be said for G. D. Kilpatrick's contention[1] that Paul went up to Jerusalem 'to *get information*' from Peter. Peter—not to mention the other Jerusalem apostles—had information to impart, tradition to transmit, testimony to relate, which Paul either did not know or (as a persecutor) knew only in a garbled version.

Can we at this time of day identify in his letters any of the 'information' Paul got from Peter during his memorable visit? This is our second question, and our answer is: 'The tradition which Paul quotes about the Resurrection of Jesus in 1 Cor. 15.3ff:

'That Christ died for our sins according to the scriptures; that he was buried; that he was raised on the third day, according to the scriptures; and that he appeared to Cephas and afterwards to the Twelve. . . . Then he appeared to over five hundred of our brothers at once. . . . Then he appeared to James, and afterwards to all the apostles.'

Why do we connect this tradition with Paul's fortnight's visit to Jerusalem?

[1] *Studies in the Gospels*, 144-149.

There are two reasons. The first—and it is one that only those with the original language will fully understand—is the presence in the Greek of 'Semitisms' — Hebrew, or Aramaic, idioms glimmering through the Greek, like the Aramaic name of Peter, the place of the ordinal 'third' after 'day', the double reference to 'the scriptures', the use of 'appeared' (*ōphthē*) corresponding to the Aramaic *'ithame*.[1]

The second is the fact that the two apostles named in the tradition—Peter and James the Lord's brother—are precisely the two whom Paul met during his fortnight's visit. This is surely more than the long arm of coincidence.

If now we remember that the fortnight's visit to Jerusalem occurred 'three years' after his conversion, probably in A.D. 35—within five years of the crucifixion of Jesus—we may see how early and important was the 'information' Paul received.

At this point someone may object that our view flatly contradicts Paul's statement seven verses earlier in his letter: 'I did not receive it (my Gospel) from man, nor was I taught it, but it came through a revelation of Jesus Christ.' But the contradiction is only apparent, not real. Paul did receive his Gospel by 'revelation', when the glorified Lord, by revealing himself to him on the Damascus road, convinced Paul that the Gospel which the Christians were preaching was true, that the crucified One was indeed the Lord of heaven. But the *historical evidence* for Christ's Ressurrection—the factual information about the first appearances of the risen one to his disciples—this must have been one fruit of the fortnight's visit. In his colloquy with Peter, Paul got his facts straight, assured himself that on these he was at one with the Jerusalem apostles, so that he could say, 'Whether then it was I or they (Peter, James, John and the rest), it is in these terms that we preach and in these terms that you believed' (I Cor. 15.11).

Paul's fortnight's visit to Jerusalem we may judge, then, to have been very much worth while. During it he secured for himself—and for Christians down nineteen centuries—what is undoubtedly the oldest and best historical evidence

[1] See J. Jeremias, *The Eucharistic Words of Jesus,* 101-103.

for the Resurrection of Jesus. It is evidence which, in the judgment of Hans Von Campenhausen[1], the distinguished German historian, 'meets all the demands of historical reliability that can possibly be made.' 'Doubt this,' he adds, 'and you might as well doubt every other statement in the New Testament—and more.'

44. 'The Law of Christ'

(Galatians 6.2)

A very unpauline phrase, surely, for Paul! Does not the apostle declare that 'Christ is the end of the law' (Rom. 10.4), meaning that with Christ in the field the law as a means of salvation is superseded and done with? Does he not sum up Christian behaviour in four words, 'Walk by the Spirit' (Gal. 5.16)? How then can he speak of himself as being 'under the law of Christ' (1 Cor. 9.21) and urge his converts to 'fulfil the law of Christ' (Gal. 6.2)? What is this law of Christ? Is Paul preparing some new sort of Christian legalism, seeking to 'build up what he once tore down' (Gal. 2.18)?

It will help towards an answer if we begin by remembering that behind Paul's Greek word for law, *nomos*, lies the Hebrew *Tōrāh*. *Tōrāh* meant divine teaching. For the Jew it signified 'all that God had made known of his nature, purpose and character and of what he would have men be and do'. Moreover, it is quite clear that Paul regarded Christ as representing, in word and deed, a new *Tōrāh*—a new revelation of God's nature and will for man.

We may now look at the two chapters where Paul speaks of 'the law of Christ'. In 1 Cor. 9.14, as in 1 Cor. 7.10, Paul authoritatively quotes 'commands' of Christ, one on the right of the preacher to get his living from the Gospel, the other on the sanctity of the marriage bond. Now turn to Gal. 6.1f

[1] *Tradition and Life in the Church*, 44f.

and note how Paul reproduces Christ's teaching about restoring an erring brother (Matt. 18.15f.) just before he bids them 'bear one another's burdens' and so 'fulfil the law of Christ'. Quite obviously for Paul obedience to the law of Christ meant carrying out his commands.

It is therefore a complete mistake to suppose that 'fulfilling the law of Christ' and 'walking by the Spirit' stand for two quite different and opposed conceptions of Christian behaviour. Paul bids his Galatian readers do both. He means that in the commands of Christ, which for short he calls 'the law of Christ', the Christian has his divinely-given pattern for the good life. On the other hand, in trying to live according to that pattern, he must use the help of God's enabling Spirit—must live by God's grace.

Grace and law—the law of Christ—therefore span the arch of Paul's Christianity. But Paul himself did not build that arch. It went back to Christ. Understand aright the Sermon on the Mount—the Sermon which begins with 'ethics of grace' (the Beatitudes)[1] and ends with a summons to put Christ's commands into practice (the parable of the Two Builders)—and you find the same arch. The truth is that Jesus was both a Saviour from sin and a teacher of righteousness; and in his great invitation to all labouring under the burden of the law of Moses (as interpreted by the scribes and Pharisees) we find both succour and demand, both grace and law. 'Come to me,' he says, 'all who labour and are heavy-laden, and I will give you rest. Take my yoke upon you (the law of Christ) and learn from me.' (Matt. 11.28f.).

What bearing has this discussion of 'the law of Christ' on our modern problems and perplexities?

Some *avant-garde* Christian moralists would persuade us that 'nothing is prescribed but love.' For the exponents of this 'new morality' rules in any shape or form seem to be 'out' and 'situational ethics' seem to be 'in'. In the old days, faced with difficult moral issues, we looked hopefully to the

[1] E.g. Matt. 5.3 'How blest are those who know their need of God' (NEB). The Beatitudes mean not that men must do these things to earn God's favour but that his blessing rests on those who feel their need of God, show mercy, are pure in heart, etc.

moral teaching of Jesus to provide us not indeed with cut-and-dried answers but with 'guide lines' to help us in making decisions. Nowadays our 'new moralists' seem to be telling us that 'love' is the only norm we need.

Two comments may suffice. First: guard their teaching, as they say, the new moralists seem to be opening the door wide to 'existential antinomianism'—the taking of moral decisions on the spur of the moment with complete disregard for any authoritative and accepted ethical standards. Second: against this new morality, it seems to us, stand both the Lord and his apostle. Neither Christ nor Paul tell us to 'love and do as you like'. On the contrary, and with realism, both see the necessity of giving counsels and laying down commandments to guide men in the Christian way.

We are not then making a plea for a new Christian legalism. We are simply insisting, with Christ and Paul, that in a fallen world 'guide lines' will always be necessary for sinful men.

45. God's Plan

(Ephesians 1.9f. RSV)

When we fell to arguing about God's ways with men in the world, an old Scots Calvinist woman of my acquaintance used to silence all doubters with the question, 'Do you think He hadn't a plan?' She might have been thinking of the Epistle to the Ephesians. In an earlier letter Paul had summed up the purpose of Christ's coming in the words, 'In Christ God was reconciling the world to himself' (2 Cor. 5.19). In Ephesians he spells out the plan.

'In Christ . . . a plan . . . to unite.' These words from the opening doxology (1.3-14) sound very modern. We might be listening in to a conference between Anglicans and Methodists about re-union. But Paul is talking about something incomparably bigger, about God's plan for humanity's

112

re-union in Christ—what Tennyson called 'the Christ that is to be'. God's purpose is unity in Christ, a unity which he designs to embrace not only the world but the cosmos.

(If he is to 'get the hang of' this profound epistle, the reader would be well advised to use a good modern translation. The long sentences and archaic English of the AV make a pretty daunting combination. The opening doxology, for instance, has no less than 258 words and includes phrases like 'the dispensation of the fullness of times' and 'the redemption of the purchased possession'. If he will turn to the NEB he will find the doxological long sentence cut up into seven short ones and the abstract nouns made as concrete as they can be.)

But now to the plan itself. Of the Epistle's six chapters the first three supply the theology, the last three the ethical issues involved. C. H. Dodd has summed up the theology in one sentence. 'It is the glory of the Church as the society which embodies in history the eternal purpose of God revealed in Christ.' Can we make that still clearer by teasing out its main ideas in three paragraphs, using Paul's own words?

The ultimate reality is 'one God and Father of all'. He 'has destined us in love to be his sons', and he purposes community for all his creatures. But the world—indeed the universe—has a great rift at its heart, with sinful men at odds and enmity with each other and superhuman powers disrupting the order God intended for his creation. That fatal rift—that estrangement and hostility—man cannot of himself repair. Only God can, and it is his purpose to subdue all evil forces —human and superhuman—so as to create a great unity.

The plan is centred in Christ. The Gospel of Christ is the good news of God's 'mystery' or unveiled secret ('mystery' here means not an enigma but a hidden purpose of God now being disclosed). This unveiled secret is embodied in Christ who is not only the Messiah of the Jews, but God's clue to the world's riddle, the integrating power of his universe. When 'the time was ripe', God put his plan into effect by sending Christ to die for men's sins, raising him from the dead and enthroning him in heaven, where he now reigns far above all possible authorities and powers. What God had in mind was nothing less than the reconciliation to himself and to one another of all his rebellious creatures.

It is through the Church that God's plan is now being progressively realised. The Church, which draws its life from Christ its ascended Head, is his working Body—the social organism designed to execute God's saving purpose among men. God the Father wills fellowship in Christ. In that fellowship 'the middle wall of partition'—the Jewish law—which once separated Gentiles from Jews, has now been broken down by Christ's sacrifice on the Cross, so that Gentiles, once 'far off' from grace and 'without hope and God in the world', are now 'fellow citizens with God's people, members of God's household'. But this healing of an old division is but prelude to something still vaster—the movement, under God, of all created beings to an ultimate unity in Christ. When this comes to pass, there will be 'a single new humanity' enjoying access through Christ to the Father and forming a great living temple for 'a habitat of God through the Spirit'.

This is the theology of Ephesians. But truth in the New Testament is always 'truth in order to goodness'. So in the second half of his letter Paul indicates how we are to live if we are to be 'worthy of our vocation' and co-workers with God in his mighty plan. The Church's marching orders are in fact four:

First: by Christian love and patience and by the use of the various gifts Christ gives us, we are to promote the Church's unity and growth.

Second: we are to 'give up living like pagans with their good-for-nothing notions'—their lusts and their lies— and 'as God's dear children, try to be like him and to live in love as Christ loved us'.

Third: we are to build Christian homes—homes where reverence for Christ will produce among the various members of the household that deference, love, honour, obedience, service and forbearance which will make the family a little miniature of the Church.

114

Fourth: in the struggle before the Church in the world we must put on the spiritual armour which God supplies. Truth, integrity, the gospel of peace, the shield of faith, the helmet of salvation, the word of God which the Spirit gives—these, with the power of prayer, are the weapons to equip Christians to fight the battle of the Lord. And the end in view is nothing less than a Christian empire growing under God until it unites all men under the sovereignty of Christ the Lord.

No book of the New Testament is more modern—more relevant to the task which confronts the Church in the world today. It holds out the inspiring vision of the Church as the working Body of Christ in the earth, and of its mission to bind all nations in a brotherhood of worship and love. It calls to men cowering behind their ideological iron-curtains and living a kind of barbed-wire existence, 'Unite—or perish!' To us who fight under Christ's banner it says, 'Onward, Christian soldiers' —

> On to the end of the road,
> On to the city of God.

46. Kenōsis

(Philippians 2.7)

The Greek verb in Phil. 2.7 (kenoun 'empty' or 'pour out') gives us kenōsis, the noun theologians have used to explain how Christ could be pre-existent and yet live on earth a truly human life. The man who first spoke of kenōsis in this way may have been the great Moravian Zinzendorff (1700-60). Seeking to declare Christ's condescension in the incarnation, he taught that, when he became man, he relinquished his divine attributes:

He left his Father's home above,
(So free, so infinite his grace)
Emptied himself of all but love
And bled for Adam's helpless race.

Charles Wesley, the author of these lines, was a friend of Zinzendorff, and 'emptied himself' is his translation of *heauton ekenōsen* in Phil. 2.7.

'Kenotic' explanations of Christ's person were once more popular than they are today. Nor is the reason far to seek. Express the idea of *kenōsis,* as many did, in terms of Christ's shedding, in the incarnation, of certain metaphysical divine attributes, and you run into all kinds of difficulties, as Donald Baillie showed in his *God was in Christ.* But 'moralise your dogma', and you may use the idea of *kenōsis* as a necessary element in any serious attempt to penetrate the mystery of Christ the God-man. 'The Son of God,' wrote P. T. Forsyth in *The Person and Place of Jesus Christ,* 'by an act of love's omnipotence set aside the style of a God and took the style of a servant and the mode of action that marks human nature.' 'Took the style of a servant': at once we think of Phil. 2.6-11 where of course Paul is not constructing a theory of Christ's person but using the *kenōsis* of Christ as a supreme incentive to Christian humility. 'Yours,' he says, 'is to be the same mind which Christ Jesus showed.' (Or perhaps, 'Have the same mind in you which you also have in your union with Christ Jesus'.)

But we are right in supposing that Phil. 2.6-11 is Paul's own creation? In 1927 the German scholar Lohmeyer piled argument on argument—from context, vocabulary, style and theology— to show that it was in fact one of the very earliest Christian hymns—a hymn being sung by Christians even before Paul began to write his letters. Since Lohmeyer's time an ever growing number of scholars have concluded that it is indeed a pre-pauline hymn to Christ. But if this is so, what is its true theme and meaning?

 The first point to seize is that *heauton ekonōsen* is a translation of the Hebrew of Isa. 53.12. It means 'he poured himself (or 'his life') out', like water from a vase, in the

116

sense of sacrificing himself. One chief clue therefore to the interpretation of the hymn is the last and greatest of Isaiah's songs about the Servant of the Lord (Isa. 52.13-53.12). Read the hymn again and notice how it is shot through with words and phrases from that passage: 'taking the form of a servant' 'he humbled himself' 'unto death' 'wherefore God highly exalted him'.

The second main clue comes in the first verse of the hymn: 'Who being in the form of God did not think equality with God something to be grasped (or 'clutched')'. Here there is clear reference to Gen. 1.26, 'Let us make man in our image' and Gen. 3.5, 'You will be like God'. In other words, the theme of the hymn is Christ the Second Adam who, conquering the temptation to which the first Adam fell, chose instead the role of the Suffering Servant of the Lord (Cf. our Lord's words in Mark 10.45) and for his obedience unto death was exalted by God the Father, that he might become Lord of all created beings.

If, using iambic trimeters, we print out the hymn in six stanzas (as Lohmeyer does), we get a hymn which might still be sung by Christians today:

> Though in God's form he was,
> Christ Jesus did not clutch
> At parity with God;
>
> Himself he sacrificed,
> Taking a servant's form,
> Being born like every man;
>
> Revealed in human shape,
> Obediently he stooped
> To die upon a cross.
>
> Him therefore God raised high,
> Gave him the name of Lord,
> All other names above;
>
> That at the Saviour's name,
> No knee might be unbowed,
> In heaven, or earth, or hell;

117

And every tongue confess,
To God the Father's praise,
That "Jesus Christ is Lord."

A. M. H.

47. Gambling and the Gospel

(Philippians 2.30)

'We must not tear this,' said the four Roman soldiers
of our Lord's seamless tunic, 'let us toss for it.' (John
19.24 NEB). Gambling at the foot of the Cross! Christian
preachers have not failed to make capital out of this. But
before we launch into a tirade against gambling—undoubtedly
one of the biggest evils in our society today—let us agree
that it was the most natural thing in the world for these
soldiers to do. Let us also remember that, when the apostles
had to decide between Joseph Barsabbas and Matthias as
a successor to Judas (who abandoned his place among the
Twelve to 'go where he belonged'), they too 'drew lots' (Acts
1.26). Them also we must exonerate, because in those days
this was one way of discovering the will of God. 'The lot
is cast into the lap,' we read in scripture (Prov. 16.33), 'but
the decision is wholly from the Lord.'

There is however another New Testament character who
gambled in a truly noble way. Epaphroditus, Paul tells the
Christians in Philippi, 'gambled with his life' in order to set
forward 'Christ's work.' (Phil. 2.30). The Greek verb which
Paul uses, *paraboleusamenos,* lit. 'throwing down a stake',
means the same as the English word 'hazard' which originally
signified a game of chance.

But Epaphroditus was not the only gambler of this kind
among the early Christians. Later, we are told, there arose
certain Christian lay brotherhoods who, because they 'hazarded' their lives to nurse cases of plague and fever, earned
for themselves the nickname of the *Parabolani* 'the Gamblers'.
Just such a gambler, last century, was Father Damien who,

118

to succour the lepers on Molokai island, gambled with his
life—and lost it. The spirit of the gambler need not be so
unethical as some strict moralists would suppose. 'I am
God's gambler,' said Kagawa of Japan, 'I have staked my
life on him.' But was there not another who, according
to Studdert-Kennedy, 'hazarded his life' for the greatest
stake of all—

> And, sitting down, they watched Him there,
> The soldiers did;
> There, while they played with dice,
> He made His Sacrifice,
> And died upon the Cross to rid
> God's world of sin.
>
> He was a gambler too, my Christ,
> He took his life and threw
> It for a world redeemed.
> And ere His agony was done,
> Before the westering sun went down,
> Crowning that day with its crimson crown,
> He knew that He had won.

48. The Goodness of the Godless

(Philippians 4.8)

We have all known, or read about, good men (like 'honest'
John Morley) who were unbelievers. How should the
Christian regard the goodness of the godless? It is a problem
that has long bothered believers. Once Christians took the
line that, unless a man held the Christian faith he was in-
capable of doing right in God's eyes. The virtues of the
pagan could then be dismissed (in Augustine's words) as
'brilliant vices'.

They might have taken another view if they had properly understood what Paul was saying in Phil. 4.8: 'All that rings true *(alēthē)*, all that commands reverence *(semna)*, and all that makes for right *(dikaia)*; all that is pure *(hagna)*, all that is attractive *(prosphilē)*, all that is high-toned *(euphēma)*; virtue *(aretē)* and merit *(epainos)*, wherever virtue and merit are found, you must take them into account *(logizesthe)*.'

Now this is not the Christian ethic, as Paul understood it. Not a mention of *agapē* or the imitation of Christ; instead we have eight Greek words (four of them not found elsewhere in Paul) which suggest not so much Christian ideals as pagan ones. These are the moral values you might have found recommended in some contemporary Greek manual of moral philosophy.

Why does Paul go out of his way to recommend pagan ethics here? Were his readers in Philippi regarding pagan excellencies around them as demonic caricatures of Christian virtues? It sounds as if they had asked him what attitude they should adopt to the good features in the pagan life with which they were surrounded. Paul's answer is a noble one. Truth is truth, whoever utters it; virtue is virtue wherever found; merit is merit whoever shows it; and you must take it into your reckoning.

Must not this be the true Christian attitude still? To be sure, in our contemporary godless society there is much that the Christian must reject out of hand. But when in our day-by-day contact with our neighbours—be they atheists, humanists or communists—we encounter goodness and truth, purity and merit, we must be quick to acknowledge it. For is not God, on the Christian view, the ultimate source of all goodness? (Mark 10.18.)

49. Faith, Love, Hope

(Colossians, 1.4 etc.)

What are the marks of the Christian life? If you had put this question to one of the first Christians, he might well have replied, 'Three—faith, love, hope'.

Seven times Paul brings these three little words together (1 Thess. 1.3, 5.8, Col. 1.4f., 1 Cor. 13.13, Gal. 5.5f., Eph. 4.2-5, Rom. 5.1-5), thrice in this order and thrice in the order we find at the end of his hymn in praise of love— 'Now abideth faith, hope, love—these three' (1 Cor. 13.13). We may surmise that 'faith, love, hope' is the original order since 'faith rests on the past, love works in the present, and hope looks to the future'.

Nonetheless, for all his use of it, it is unlikely that Paul invented the triad. The evidence suggests it was one of the many things Paul received from his Christian predecessors. Note, first, how Paul describes it 'Faith, hope, love, these three', as though it were a formula already familiar to his readers. Second, very significantly, when Paul mentions two of the three words, he is involuntarily driven, as in 1 Thess. 5.8, to include the third, 'love', though it mars the symmetry of his picture. Finally, the triad keeps cropping up in other early Christian documents like 1 Peter, Hebrews and a letter of Polycarp, as though it were something out of the common Christian pool and not the apostle's own collocation. Modern scholars therefore hold that it is 'a primitive Christian triad'. (One later Christian writer, Macarius, even traces it back to Jesus. 'Take care of faith and hope,' he quotes the Lord as saying, 'through which is begotten the love of God and of man which gives eternal life.')

Dean Inge once said that if we could discover what the earliest Christians meant by such little words as faith, hope and love, we should find ourselves at the very heart of the

Christian revelation. Happily, to guide us in our quest, we have Paul's own exegesis of them, notably in 1 Thess. 1.3 (where he combines them with 'work' 'labour' and 'endurance') and, above all, in Col. 1.4f. 'Your faith in Christ Jesus . . . the love which you have for all the saints . . . the hope which is laid up for you in heaven.'

For Paul faith (*pistis*) means taking God at his saving word in Christ. Directed not to a proposition but to a person, faith is utter trust in the living Christ who 'died for our sins' and now lives and reigns as King and Head of the Church, which is his Body.

Next, according to Paul, 'faith works through love' (Gal. 5.6). Love is *agapē*, the love which seeks not to possess but to give, to spend and be spent for the object beloved. It is the energy which Christians are called to radiate among their fellow men, and its exemplar is Christ's own love.

And, lastly, 'hope' (*elpis*) is the confidence that the God who has redeemed men in the Cross will, at the end, reward his faithful people with the glory 'laid up for them in heaven.'

If this is the essence of the earliest Christianity, we may define Christians as those who live by faith—that kind of faith, work through love—that kind of love, and abide in hope —that kind of hope. Are not these the marks of true Christians still?

50. Paregorics

(Colossians 4.11)

When Paul said that his three friends Aristarchus, Mark and Jesus Justus had been 'a comfort' to him in his imprisonment, he used a doctor's word, *parēgoria,* which has passed into our language as 'paregoric'. Hippocrates (460-359 B.C), the most celebrated physician of antiquity (whose name still survives in 'the Hippocratic oath') had employed the word for a medicine that alleviates pain. More than a century after Christ the Greek physician Galen (A.D. 130-201), medical adviser to Marcus Aurelius and the doctor who first diagnosed by the pulse, used *parēgoria* in the same way. So, when we read three verses later in Colossians, that Luke 'the beloved physician' was in Paul's company as he was writing, the natural surmise is that Paul got the word from his doctor friend.

Our modern translators are content to follow the AV and render it 'comfort' which has no medical overtones. A word which has, is 'tonic'. 'These men', Paul says, 'I have found a tonic.' To be sure, 'tonic' suggests a 'pick-me-up' rather than a pain-killer. On the other hand, we may be sure that the three friends who had 'comforted' Paul in prison had not only assuaged his anxieties but had, like a tonic, given him vigour and strength.

If there are people in the world who add to the sum of its pain, there are mercifully others whose blessed gift it is to be paregorics—people who not only (in Carlyle's phrase) 'wrap up our bleeding moods in the softest of bandages' but impart 'pep' and 'tonic' to our run-down spirits. God send us all in our hour of need friends who will act on us as paregorics.

51. 'Test all Things'

(1 Thessalonians 5.21f.)

The counterfeiting of coins must be almost as old as human duplicity; and, to counter the counterfeiting, the money-changers down the centuries have devised their own ways of testing a coin to see whether it be true or false. (Not so very long ago, when gold sovereigns were still in currency, one rough and ready test was to bite them!) In New Testament times what the moneychanger did was to drop the dubious coin on a table with a glass top, and the sound it made enabled his expert ear to determine whether it was good or bad money. That our Lord had seen moneychangers doing this—probably at Passover time when pilgrims, up for the feast, had to exchange their *denars* or their *drachmas* for the required half shekel of temple tax—is proved by something he once said.

Scholars speak of the *Agrapha* ('unwritten things'). The term refers to those sayings of Jesus which are not found in the New Testament but have come down to us mostly in the works of early Church fathers but sometimes on scraps of papyrus exhumed from the sands of old Egypt. Of all these 'unfamiliar sayings' of Jesus perhaps the most frequently quoted one is this: 'Show yourselves tried (*dokimoi*) money-changers, rejecting (*apodokimazontes*) much, but retaining (*katechontes*) the good (*kalon*)'.

The words obviously recall the world of the moneychanger and his need to discriminate between true and false coins. *Dokimazein* is the Greek verb for 'assaying' or 'testing' metals. Add the prefix *apo* and you get *apodokimazein* which means to 'reject' after testing. The adjective *dokimos* signifies 'tested' or 'tried'.

But is this saying of Jesus really an *Agraphon*? Does it not in fact occur in the New Testament?

Students of Paul know how on occasion he refers to sayings of Jesus in order to settle questions of Christian behaviour or practice (see 1 Cor. 7.10 and 9.14). Sometimes however in the 'practical' sections of his letters, e.g. Rom. 12-14, he echoes words of the Lord without an explicit, 'As the Lord said'. So it is in the last chapter of First Thessalonians. Echoes of Christ's words can be heard in his simile about the day of the Lord 'coming like a thief in the night' (Cf. Matt. 24.43), in his precept 'Be at peace among yourselves' (Cf. Mark 9.50) and in the command, 'See that none of you repays evil for evil' (Cf. Matt. 5.44). But it is his last piece of advice which concerns us here:

'[19]Do not quench the Spirit, [20]do not despise prophesying, [21]but test (*dokimazete*) everything; hold fast (*katechete*) what is good (*kalon*), [22]abstain from every form (*eidous*) of evil (*ponerou*)' (1 Thess. 5.19-22 RSV). The strong similarity of vv. 21f. to the 'unfamiliar saying' of Jesus can hardly be fortuitous. Commentators ancient and modern have noted it and rightly concluded that Paul was echoing a word of his Lord.

But is the RSV's 'form of evil' a right rendering of the Greek phrase *eidous ponērou*? *Ponērou* is treated as an abstract noun. But the analogy of Job 1.1, 8 and the fact that the definite article is lacking, suggest that it is an adjective qualifying *eidous*. The meaning of *eidos* is really the crux of the matter. You may give it, as the RSV does, the quasi-philosophical sense of 'form'. But this meaning, common in Plato, does not occur in the New Testament. Again, you may translate, as the AV does, 'appearance of evil'; but the connexion with vs. 21 ('test all things') seems to rule this meaning out. Or you may, as the NEB does, assign *eidos* the meaning it often has in the papyri, 'kind', and render 'avoid the bad of whatever kind'. But perhaps the likeliest meaning of all emerges if you connect *eidos,* as there is linguistic warrant for doing, with the *die* or stamp used in making coins and the resultant 'pattern' impressed on them. The Latin equivalent of *eidos* is *species* from which we get our English 'specie' which means coined money. *Eidous ponerou* will therefore signify 'bad money', and we may paraphrase 1 Thess. 5.21f. something like this: '(Like expert money-changers) test everything: keep the good metal, and refuse the spurious coin'.

We may now return to the situation in Thessalonica. Paul applies his Lord's saying to the problem of distinguishing between true and dubious prophesyings. It was a problem which vexed the early Church a good deal. Some men, when they got up to prophesy in church meetings, uttered Christian truth; others simply vapoured; and there were still others whose pronouncements might be heretical or even dangerous. Would not a ban on all prophesying be the best thing? Paul answered with characteristic sanity. 'Don't,' he says in effect, 'quench the fire of the Spirit. Let them go on prophesying, but don't regard all their pronouncements as revelations from on high. Bring all to the test of the Christian conscience which is sensitive to what is *kalon*—"genuine"—and reject all that does not ring true—true to Christ and the Gospel.'

125

In our day we still have many who prophesy in the name of Christ, whether they pronounce from pulpits, or commit their pronouncements to paper, or peddle their 'gospels' from door to door. There are Christian 'deviationists'—Jehovah's Witnesses, Seventh Day Adventists and the rest. There are preachers who offer their hearers pale emasculated versions of the historic Gospel—'half Gospels' as P. T. Forsyth called them, 'with no dignity and no future'—'like the famous mule having neither pride of ancestry nor hope of posterity'. And there are *avant-garde* Christian 'prophets' today who, seeking to accommodate Christianity to the spirit of the age, trick out the Gospel in the, often alien, categories of some contemporary and fashionable philosophy. What is to be our attitude to all these? The answer in Paul's words—and he is echoing Christ—is this: 'Bring each and every one of them to the test: keep what is good and genuine in them, but, where necessary, expose them for the shams and counterfeits they are'.

Elsewhere in 1 Cor. 12.2f., Paul tells us what his own touchstone is: 'No one can say, "Jesus is Lord" except by the Holy Spirit'. In other words, any Gospel which exalts Jesus, which calls him *Kyrios* (Lord), which sets him on that side of reality we call divine, is genuine. (Paul would have been the first to test this assertion by the fruit of the confessor's life.) Any Gospel which does not do this is to be rejected.

52. The Sure Sayings

(1 Timothy 1.15 etc.)

Four times (or possibly five[1]) in the Pastoral Epistles (1 and 2 Timothy and Titus) which, if they do not wholly come from the pen of St. Paul, are certainly 'Pauline', we light on the formula *Pistos ho logos*. The AV translates it 'Faithful is the

[1] 1 Tim. 3.1, is not certainly a 'faithful saying'; for some MSS here read *anthrōpinos* (not *pistos*) which gives the NEB's 'It is a popular saying'.)

saying', and the RSV 'The saying is sure'. The phrase
evidently marks a quotation, and introduces something which
the early Christians believed was of the essence of Christian
faith and practice. Indeed, when we examine the sayings, most
have a clear rhythm, suggesting that they embody early Christian confessions of faith or are snatches of Christian hymns,
which have their roots in what Christ had said and done.

A brief study of these 'sure sayings' may be useful if only
to compare what the early Christians thought belonged to
the substance of the Faith with what the *avant garde* theologians of today regard as being of its essence.

The first one (1 Tim. 1.15) reads: 'The saying is sure and
worthy of full acceptance, that Christ Jesus came into the
world to save sinners' (RSV). However men have pictured
Jesus down the centuries—and their portraits have been many
and diverse—the early Christians regarded him pre-eminently
as a Saviour from sin. This was the heart of their *Credo*—
'Christ died for our sins' (1 Cor. 15.3). They believed that he
came, not so much to preach the Atonement, as that there
might be an atonement to preach. And they had good warrant
for this belief in the words of Jesus himself. 'I did not come
to invite virtuous people (into God's Kingdom)' he said, 'but
sinners' (Mark 2.17 NEB). 'The Son of man,' he told
Zaccheus, 'came to seek and save the lost' (Luke 19.10). His
ministry of service was to be crowned by his giving his life
'as a ransom for many' (Mark 10.45).

The second 'sure saying', in 1 Tim. 4.9, probably refers not
to what follows it but to what goes before: 'Godliness (the
Greek is *eusebeia*, best rendered 'religion') is of value in every
way, as it holds promise for the present life and also for the
life to come' (RSV). It is an answer to the question, What is
the use of 'religion'? What it means is not (though some have
thought it open to this interpretation) that religion helps a
man to 'make the best of both worlds', but that it promises
life (*zoē*)—real life, life that is life indeed, life lived in the
presence of God—both here and hereafter. There is a recorded
saying of Jesus, introduced by one of his solemn Amens,
which said something very like this (Luke 18.30).

The third 'sure saying' (2 Tim. 2.11) is quite clearly a verse

127

from a baptismal hymn. (Cf. Rom. 6.4 'We were buried with him by baptism into death that, as Christ was raised from the dead by the glory of his Father, we too might walk in newness of life'.) So plainly rhythmical are the words that they almost set themselves to music, and we are warranted, when translating, in turning them into verse:

> If we with Him have died,
> With Him to life we rise,
> If we but firm endure,
> A throne with Him our prize.

> But let us Him deny,
> Deny us too must He:
> Though we may faithless prove,
> Yet faithful will He be.

Once again the early Christians had dominical warrant for this in what Jesus himself had said: 'Everyone who acknowledges me before men, I will also acknowledge before my Father who is in heaven; but whoever denies me before men, I will also deny before my Father who is in heaven.' (Matt. 10.32f.). 'He who endures to the end will be saved.' (Mark 13.13).

The fourth 'sure saying' comes in Titus 3.8. Here the reference is probably to the two verses which precede the formula: 'The Holy Spirit which God poured out richly upon us through Jesus Christ our Saviour, so that we might be justified by his grace and become heirs in hope of eternal life.' The rhythm and heightened tone in these words suggest a piece of early Christian liturgy—or perhaps catechesis—but they sum up the Gospel of God's justification, by grace through faith, of sinners, which it was Paul's glory and delight (and not his alone) to preach.

What then do the 'sure sayings' of the Pastoral Epistles add up to? The worth of religion for life, the Saviourhood of Christ, the call to Christian fidelity and fortitude, the good news of God's grace to sinners in Christ and the blessed hope of eternal life. For the early Christians these were among 'the things most surely believed'.

How stands the case today? We live in an age when the

demand is for 'religionless Christianity' and when some advanced Christian theologians would like to 'demythologise the Gospel' and re-write its central tenets in terms which will be acceptable to sceptical, irreligious and scientifically-minded modern man. For them 'religion' is a 'dirty word'; their doxology would seem to be 'Glory to man in the depths of his being'; they invite us to see in Jesus 'the man for others'; and they sum up Christian morals in 'Love, and what you will, do'. These evidently are the 'sure words' of the so-called 'new theology'. Compare these slogans with the 'sure words' of the Pastorals, and must we not agree with Karl Barth that this is 'flat tyre theology'? (By this he meant that the *pneuma*—the Greek word for both 'air' and 'Spirit'—had been taken out of it.)

NB

NB.

53. Paul as Punster

(Philemon 11)

Dr Johnson has been credited with saying that 'he who would make a pun would pick a pocket' and even if this is but a garbled version of something said by someone else (John Dennis) about 'a *vile* pun', punning and word-play are disesteemed in our best literary circles. John Donne and Charles Lamb, to be sure, loved puns; but, for the most part, we have relegated the pun to the realms of the merely facetious, and we greet even a good one with a hoot of laughter.

The men of the Bible set a much higher value on word-play. Prophets did not scorn to use it. 'Jeremiah, what do you see?' said the Lord to the prophet. 'I see a rod of almond' (Hebrew *shaqēd*). 'You have seen well, for I am watching over (*shaqēd*) my word to perform it.' The almond tree gets its name from the fact that it is the first tree to 'awake' when the winter is over. Jeremiah, noting its buds, sees in them a sign that the Lord is 'awake' and active (Jer. 1.11f.).

But we have a higher warrant for word-play than this. According to Matt. 16.18, our Lord himself indulged in it at

Caesarea Philippi. After Peter had confessed him to be the Messiah, he said, 'You are *Kephā,* and on this *Kephā* I will build my church'. *Kephā* is Aramaic for 'rock', the Greek equivalent being *petra.* Unfortunately the pun is concealed in English, though it comes through in German: 'You are rock (*Fels*), and on this rock (*Felsen*) I will build my church'.

Nor did the apostle shrink from playing on words. In his little letter to Philemon Paul deliberately plays on the name of the runaway slave Onesimus whose cause he is pleading. By derivation Onesimus means in Greek 'useful', 'profitable'. 'I appeal to you,' writes Paul to Philemon, the slave's former master, 'for the child of my imprisonment, Onesimus. Once he was useless (*achrēston*) to you, but now he is very useful (*euchrēston*) both to you and to me.' Nor did Paul's punning appeal fail, for we have reason to believe not only that Philemon forgave and took back his thieving runaway (now a Christian) but that Onesimus rose to become a beloved bishop in the church of Ephesus.[1]

It has been said that in the mouth of Charles Lamb the pun, so far from being a mere piece of verbal dexterity, could become 'a sudden glory of revealed truth'. Is this not also true of the Bible? Jeremiah, playing on words, can find in a 'waking' almond tree the token of a 'waking' God; our Lord, on a supreme occasion, can pun on Peter's name; and his apostle can include a most effective word-play in what has been called 'the most gentlemanly letter ever written'.[2]

54. Hope the Anchor

(Hebrews 6.19)

'Will your anchor hold in the storms of life?' begins Priscilla Owens' hymn which The Boys' Brigade have made their own. (By no stretch of the literary imagination can it be called a

---

[1] *The Epistle of Ignatius to the Ephesians,* 1.3, 'Onesimus, a man of inexpressible love, and your bishop'.

[2] The phrase is 'Rabbi' Duncan's.

great hymn; its appeal lies rather in the image of the anchor and its inspiriting tune.) This nineteenth century Priscilla took her metaphor from Heb. 6.19. Curiously enough, some good modern scholars believe this book was written by Priscilla, the wife of Aquila and the friend of Paul and, by all the evidence of the New Testament, a most notable Christian woman. (In four out of the six New Testament references to the couple the wife's name comes first.)

Heb. 6.19 apart, the only other New Testament reference to anchors comes in Acts 28, 'the Sailors' Chapter', which recounts Paul's voyage to Rome. On the day before the shipwreck on Malta, Dr Luke tells us, 'as we were drifting across the sea of Adria about midnight the sailors suspected that they were nearing land . . . and fearing that we might run on the rocks, they let down four anchors from the stern and prayed for day to come'.

'Anchor' derives from the Greek *agkura*, the Latin *ancora*, with the meaning 'bend' or 'hook'. Doubtless there was a Hebrew word for anchor—Solomon's fleet of ships cannot have been 'anchor-less'—but the Old Testament does not mention it. Not the Hebrews but the Greeks and the Phoenicians were the great sailors of the Biblical world, the men who made and used anchors. The first ones, we are told, were large stones. Later they took to fashioning them out of wood in a hooked shape, which they weighted with metal. The familiar anchor with its double fluke (or prong)—*bidens*, 'two-toothed' the Romans called it—is said to have been the invention of one Anacharsis, about 600 B.C.

It was an easy transition from the manufacture of anchors to the making of metaphors about them, and for this the Greeks had a liking. 'It is good to have two anchors,' they said as we say it is good to have 'two strings to one's bow'. Sophocles declared that children were a mother's 'anchor'. And in what is perhaps the most famous of all the Greek images about anchors, the philosopher Pythagoras (who so influenced Plato) said that there were anchors—and anchors. 'Wealth is a frail anchor. Frailer still is fame.' 'What are the strong ones?' he asked, and gave the noble answer, 'Wisdom, magnanimity and courage'.

How then did the anchor, a Greek symbol for some kind of human stability in a stormy world, become the symbol of divine hope and immortality? 'Christ died on the Tree,' Carlyle told Emerson as they walked the Galloway moors together. 'That built Dunscore kirk yonder.' In the same way it was the Cross on the hill and the empty tomb—it was Christ crucified, risen and ascended—that turned the anchor into a symbol of deathless hope.

So we come back to the Epistle to the Hebrews. Its nautical language plus the fact that the author's name has apparently been suppressed have led some to think that the writer must have been Priscilla who certainly had sailed much on Mediterranean seas. ('Nonsense,' retorts a German critic, 'there is no evidence that Aquila was cursed with a learned wife.') Perhaps a likelier guess at the author's name was Luther's— Apollos from Alexandria was his candidate for the honour. The truth is that nobody knows his—or her—name, and our scholars are content to conceal their ignorance by calling him *Auctor,* the Latin for author. Our interest here, however, is not *Auctor's* name but *Auctor's* anchor.

We Christians, he tells us, are the true heirs of God's promise of salvation made long ago to Abraham. It has been fulfilled for us by Christ's atoning death for sin upon the Cross—that perfect sacrifice of his sinless life which he offered once for all in the heavenly Holy of Holies and which has opened for us 'a new and living way' into the very presence of God. It is this priestly 'work' of Christ on our behalf which underpins our immortal hope. 'We have this as a sure and steadfast anchor of the soul,' he says, 'a hope which enters into the inner sanctuary behind the veil where Jesus has gone as a forerunner on our behalf' (Heb. 6.19f.).

Christ's sacrifice, then, is an anchor which not only holds us in the storms of this world but ties and tethers us to the unseen one. We stand, you and I, between two worlds—the present one and the world to come. But the anchor of Christian hope, founded on Christ's sacrifice, penetrates the veil which separates the unseen world from our eyes and is fastened on the farther side. We are anchored not in time but in eternity— that eternity into which Christ, 'the pioneer and perfecter of

faith', has already entered. And where he has gone, we too
may follow—if we will but cling to the anchor which he has
made fast for us in the heavenly world.

So, after all, Priscilla Owens was not far from *Auctor's*
thought when she invited us to answer the last question in
her hymn:

> Will you anchor safe by the heavenly shore
> When life's storms are past for evermore?

with the ringing refrain:

> We have an anchor that keeps the soul,
> Steadfast and sure while the billows roll,
> Fastened to the rock which cannot move,
> Grounded firm and deep in the Saviour's love.

55. Faith as the Title-deeds

(Hebrews 11.1)

What does the writer to the Hebrews mean when, at the
beginning of his famous eleventh chapter, he defines faith as
'the *substance* of things hoped for' (AV)?

The Greek noun *hypostasis* (Latin, *substantia,* English,
'substance') means literally 'that which stands beneath', and
so 'foundation' or 'support'. From this flow various derived
meanings. For a philosopher it may mean 'essence' or 'reality'
(Compare Heb. 1.3). Since there is nothing like a firm foundation for giving a man confidence, it may also mean 'assurance'
(Cf. Heb. 3.14). And in legal and commercial usage the word
may carry the 'real estate' meaning of 'property'. Which of
these meanings best fits Heb. 11.1?

Does the Writer mean that 'faith gives substance to our
hopes' in the sense of creating the reality we hope for? This
might suggest the 'pragmatism' of the American philosopher,
William James. 'Believe that life *is* worth living,' he said, 'and
your belief will help create the fact.' But our Writer was

certainly no 'pragmatist': it was his conviction that the unseen realities exist prior to, and independently of, any human faith.

Does he mean that our faith makes us confident of what we hope for hereafter? The psychological meaning is widely accepted today. Thus the RSV translates: 'Faith is the assurance of things hoped for, the conviction of things not seen'. Undoubtedly it makes good sense, and perhaps we should content ourselves with it and look no farther.

But is it possible that the meaning of *hypostasis* here is neither philosophical nor psychological but legal? In the Greek papyri written in Egypt about the time of Christ, the word could mean 'property' in what we might call 'the Forsyte sense'. In fact, it could be applied to a collection of legal documents bearing on the ownership of a piece of property. This was the meaning preferred for Heb. 11.1 by the great expert on New Testament Greek, J. H. Moulton.

Among the papyri, for example, we find the petition of a widow called Dionysia. The poor woman, evidently plagued with law-suits about her property, had eventually bundled together all her 'papers' and sent them with her petition to the Prefect at Alexandria. As the word *hypostasis* is used in her petition, it means what we call 'title-deeds'.

'Now faith is the title-deeds of things hoped for.' It is a very attractive suggestion. We have not yet seen our future inheritance—what Heb. 11.16 calls 'a better country, a heavenly one'—but we have God's promise in the Gospel, and our faith is the title-deeds of our promised inheritance. If we do not lose them, one day, by the mercy of God, we shall see it and possess it.

56. By Faith or by Works?

(James 2.24)

How do I, a sinner, get right with God? By faith or by works? It is a very old question much debated down the centuries; and if you consult the New Testament, you find, apparently, two diametrically opposite answers to it. 'A man,' says Paul, 'is justified by faith apart from works (Rom. 3.24). 'A man,' says James, 'is justified by works and not by faith alone' (James 2.24). How are we to explain this contradiction?

The late Dr Joad's opening gambit applies here: 'It all depends upon what you mean by "faith" and "works" '. Nor are the answers doubtful. For Paul 'faith' is utter trust in, and obedience towards, Jesus Christ, God's Son, who came to save us from our sins. On the other hand, the 'faith' on which James comes down like a hammer is barren orthodoxy, mere assent to the proposition that 'God is one'. So too with the other key word 'works'. By 'works' Paul means 'works of the Law', the meritorious observance of the hundred and one precepts of the Law of Moses. By 'works' James means the lovely deeds of practical religion, Christian *agapē*, or love in action:

'Suppose a brother or sister is in rags with not enough food for the day, and one of you says, "Good luck to you, keep yourselves warm, and have plenty to eat", but does nothing to supply their bodily needs, what is the good of that? So with faith: if it does not lead to action, it is in itself a lifeless thing' (James 2.15-17 NEB).

The fact is that Paul and James are fighting on two quite different battlefields. When Paul declares that a man is justified by God's grace through faith, he is fighting against the Jews' inveterate confidence in works of 'merit', the whole scheme of belief that a man, by doing such 'works', can earn his salvation by laying up a credit balance of good works in the ledgers of heaven. James, on the other hand, is attacking the men who claim that they are saved because they hold orthodox beliefs about God—are good monotheists. (So are the devils, he comments grimly!) What rouses James's ire, making him a kind of New Testament Amos, is the dreary and dead orthodoxy which does not make the slightest difference to a man's way of living. For him, faith is only faith if it issues in what we call 'Christian Action'.

(Here we may usefully observe that both Paul and James can appeal to the teaching of their common Lord. When Paul says 'the ungodly ones are justified', he is but repeating what Jesus says in the first Beatitude, 'The beggars before God are blessed' (Matt. 5.3). When James says that 'faith without works is dead' (James 2.20), he is repeating Jesus' word in Matt. 7.21 'Not everyone who calls me "Lord, Lord" will enter the kingdom of Heaven but only those who do the will of my heavenly Father.')

In short, when you discover what Paul and James mean by 'faith' and 'works' and understand on what very different fields they are fighting, the apparent contradiction between them dwindles almost to vanishing point. Conceivably James was inveighing against some current caricature of Paul's teaching which held that faith was everything and the kind of life which accompanied it of no importance for man's salvation. The name of this heresy is Antinomianism. It has plagued the Church from Paul's day to ours. And by such heretics it has ever been supposed that what Christ did on the Cross absolves them from all obligation to 'fulfil the law of Christ' or bear the Cross themselves. Yet how monstrous a caricature it is of the apostle's doctrine anyone can see for himself merely by reading 1 Cor. 13 or Rom. 12. Set 1 Cor. 13.2 alongside James 2.26 and the alleged discord may be seen for the chimaera it really is. 'As the body apart from the spirit is dead,' says James, 'so faith apart from works is dead.' 'If I have all faith so as to remove mountains,' says Paul, 'but have not love, I am nothing.'

The sum of the matter is that, though Paul and James mean different things by 'faith' and 'works', they do not disagree on fundamentals. For James would have agreed with Paul that 'faith works through love' (Gal. 5.6), as Paul would have agreed with James that 'faith without works is dead', and both would have concurred that 'the first thing to do with faith is to live by it'.

57. 'Aliens on Earth'

(1 Peter 2.11)

Few of us think of 'parishioners' as pilgrims; and yet our word 'parish' comes from the word *paroikia* which in the Greek Bible (i.e. the Septuagint and the New Testament) means 'sojourning', or, more precisely, the life and status of a 'resident alien'. The 'sojourner' or 'alien' is a *paroikos*. Both words have legal and political origins and connotations.

In classical Greek—in writers like Sophocles and Thucydides—*paroikos,* which comes from *para* 'beside' and *oikos* 'a dwelling', meant a 'neighbour'. But in the centuries just before Christ it came to denote a non-citizen—an alien living in a foreign land and lacking the full rights of a native. The usual Hebrew word for this man was *gēr*; and when the Old Testament was translated into Greek at Alexandria, *paroikos* was a natural rendering for *gēr.* Thus, according to the Septuagint, Moses in Midian says, 'I am a *paroikos*—an alien—in a foreign land' (Exod. 2.22); and the author of the 119th Psalm speaks of 'this house of my pilgrimage' (*paroikia*) and confesses, 'I am a *paroikos*—a stranger—in the earth' (Ps. 119.19, 54). Not only so, but for the Hebrews, Israel herself is a *paroikos*—a pilgrim People of God. 'We are strangers (*paroikoi*) before thee,' says King David speaking of Israel before God, 'as all our fathers were' (1 Chron. 29.15).

Here we have the background for the New Testament use of our two words which occur half a dozen times in it. The meaning 'resident alien' comes out in Paul's speech at Pisidian Antioch. 'Our fathers', he says, 'were living as aliens in the land of Egypt' (Acts 13.17 NEB). But in Peter's first epistle it is not the legal but the spiritual meaning of the words that is primary. 'Aliens on earth,' he calls his readers (1 Peter 2.11 NEB): followers of Christ having their true homeland in

137

heaven, though they sojourn on earth. He begs them to 'live out their time on it' in a manner worthy of those whose fatherland is above (1 Peter 1.17).

But for the theology of *paroikia* (if we may so call it) the New Testament book *par excellence* is Hebrews. Its writer speaks of the Old Testament heroes of faith as 'strangers or passing travellers on earth—men who longed for a better country—the heavenly one' (Heb. 11.13ff NEB), whose hope has now at last been fulfilled in the Gospel. 'They did not enter upon their promised inheritance,' he tells us, 'because, with us in mind, God had made a better plan, that only in company with us should they reach their perfection' (Heb. 11.40 NEB). The same 'pilgrim' note rings out again superbly a century or two later in the lovely *Epistle to Diognetus*: 'Christians,' the writer says, 'dwell in their own fatherlands as if they were sojourners (*paroikoi*) in them. . . . They sojourn (*paroikousin*) among corruptible things, waiting for the incorruptibility which is in heaven' (*Ep. to Diogn.* 5.5 and 6.8).

In our time we have had no better expositor of this 'traveller's theology' than Karl Ludwig Schmidt, the famous German professor who contributed the article on *paroikos* to the well-known *Theological Dictionary of the New Testament*. In the early 'thirties when the Dictionary first began to appear, Schmidt's criticism of them incurred the disfavour of the Nazis, who deposed him from his chair in Bonn, expelled him from his fatherland, and stripped him of his citizenship; so that, by a poignant irony of history, when he finished his article on *paroikos* for the Dictionary, he had himself become one—in Switzerland.

If we are to be true to the New Testament, Schmidt said, the *ecclēsia* must never lose the note of *paroikia*—the Church of Christ must ever be a Pilgrim Church. It is something that is ever needing to be said. Who will affirm that such doctrine is popular today? Any Church leader who began a pastoral letter to the faithful with 'Dear Pilgrims on earth' would at once call down on himself the contemptuous reactions of all who dismiss the Church as an anachronistic irrelevancy. 'Otherworldliness' has gone out of fashion: 'this-worldliness'

138

and 'with-itness' are everything. Even the faithful no longer delight to sing:

> I'm but a pilgrim here
> Heaven is my home.

And on every hand we are told that, if the Church's witness is to be effective, it must not only speak the language of the time but address itself to man's economic and other needs, by attacking poverty, combatting racism, and doing all it can to serve suffering humanity.

Of course it must; and we do not need the Church's critics to tell us that there have been times in her history when a one-sided other-worldliness led her to neglect her mission to the world. But if the Church has a duty to make the woes of the world more endurable for sick and sinful men and women, has it not also a duty to make the other world—the Jerusalem which is above—more real to them? She is summoned not only to be the Body of Christ in this world, but also to keep ringing in men's ears the note of a Pilgrim Church,

> Singing songs of expectation,
> Marching to the Promised Land.

And is it not also true that down the Christian centuries God's best servants—from Paul of Tarsus to the good Pope John—have been men who, while insisting that we must live on earth as those whose true home is in heaven, have done more than most to set forward the Church's saving mission in this world? Was it not the man who wrote 'We are a colony of heaven' (Phil. 3.20 Moffatt) who did most in the first century to set 'the holy fire' of the Gospel blazing in the earth? And was it not Angelo Roncalli, Pope John, the Christian pilgrim whose last words were, 'My bags are packed. I am ready to go', who did more than any other to renew and revitalise the Church of Rome in our time and (as somebody has put it) 'made the Vatican a target of love'? 'Go home,' he said to the delegates to the Second Vatican Council which he had summoned, 'and make love grow—from here to there.'

58. 'Joint Heirs of the Grace of Life'

(1 Peter 3.7)

Is it not a little ironical that when our liturgical experts select scripture-readings for marriage services they have a way of directing us to Paul and ignoring Peter? Paul never had a wife and by the evidence of his 'It is better to marry than to burn' (1 Cor. 7.9) regarded marriage as a second best. But Peter was a married man (Mark 1.30) who took his wife around with him on his apostolic journeys (1 Cor. 9.5). Is it not arguable that Peter's practical experience of Christian marriage gave him a better title to speak to others about it than one who wrote, 'To the unmarried and the widowed I say that it is well for them to remain single as I do' (1 Cor. 7.8)?

To be sure, the young woman who jibs at the word 'obey' in the marriage service will bridle at Peter's insistence that in a home the husband should be head of the house and that the wife should recognise the fact. But, granted that Peter is no modern sex-equalitarian, do not his words to wives have their own truth and beauty:

'Wives, be submissive to your husbands so that some, though they do not obey the word, may be won without a word by the behaviour of their wives when they see your reverent and chaste behaviour. Let not yours be the outward adorning with braiding of hair, decoration of gold, and wearing of robes; but let it be the hidden person of the heart with the imperishable jewel of a gentle and quiet spirit, which in God's sight is very precious.' (1 Peter 3.1-4 RSV).

Shall we cavil at Peter's contention that the Christian wife's charm should be that of character rather than of 'make up'? Indeed, what true daughter of Sarah (to use Peter's language) would not aspire after 'the imperishable jewel of a gentle and quiet spirit'—a spirit which neither worries other people nor allows itself to be worried?

Now hear what Peter has to say to the husbands: 'Likewise you husbands, live considerately with your wives bestowing honour on the woman as the weaker sex, since you are joint heirs of the grace of life, in order that your prayers may not be hindered.' (1 Peter 3.7 RSV).

Here we have the very essence of Christian chivalry backed up by a good Gospel reason—'since you are joint heirs of the grace of life'. It is one of the most exquisite phrases in the whole New Testament. 'The grace of life' means 'God's gracious gift of life eternal'. It is a synonym for salvation.

But why does Peter add, 'In order that your prayers may not be hindered'? Because he realises that where friction between husband and wife causes heart hardening in the highest of human relationships, any relationship with God through prayer must be seriously impaired and impeded. Christian experience proclaims him right. If we may borrow some words from Burns (who must have known this from sad experience) 'a correspondence fixed with Heaven' can only subsist on 'the sacred lowe o' weel-placed love'.

59. *Koinōnia*

(1 John 1.3, 7 etc.)

Sir Edwin Hoskyns, the celebrated Cambridge Biblical scholar (1884-1937) once spoke of burying oneself in a lexicon and arising in the presence of God. He meant that with some New Testament words you may begin your study at an everyday level and find yourself, at its ending, confronted with the deepest secrets of Christian faith and experience.

Such a word is *koinōnia* which occurs 18 times in the New Testament and is variously translated 'partnership', 'communion', 'fellowship'. The root meaning of *koinōnia* is 'sharing', as the verb *koinōneō* means 'share in' and *koinōnōs* 'one who goes shares with you', i.e. a partner.

In the Greek-speaking world of our Lord's time *koinōnia* was very much a business man's word. Study the papyrus letters from Egypt written in the colloquial Greek of the age, 'the *Koiné*', and you find that it commonly means a business 'partnership'. But it can also mean a marital 'partnership' in which two people elect to share life together. Sometimes in the New Testament *koinōnia* and its cognate words bear a similar practical, everyday meaning. St. Luke can call James and John, Peter's 'partners' *(koinonoi)* (Luke 5.10) in the fishing trade; and St. Paul can apply the word to the 'collection' he was taking up for the poor Christians in the Mother Church at Jerusalem (Rom. 15.26, 2 Cor. 9.13).

I

But of course the New Testament has its own way of conscripting these everyday words into the service of the Gospel, so that *koinōnia* comes to express the deepest secret of the Christian religion—'fellowship' with God, or Christ, or the Holy Spirit—that 'fellowship' in which the great initiative always lies on the divine side, so that our communion with God always depends on his communion with us[1].

St. John can declare, 'Our fellowship is with the Father and with his Son Jesus Christ' (1 John 1.3); and St. Paul can not only say of the sacrament of the Lord's Supper, 'The bread which we break is it not a means of sharing *(koinōnia)* in the body of Christ' (1 Cor. 10.16) but even speak of 'the fellowship of the Holy Spirit' (Phil. 2.1. Cf. 2 Cor. 13.14) which we take to mean 'the fellowship which the Holy Spirit creates.'

Thus the word *koinōnia* in the New Testament has two orientations—a vertical and a horizontal—and behind it lies the whole story of Christ and his followers and the experience of the apostolic Church.

II

All began in Galilee when Jesus 'appointed twelve men, to be with him' (Mark 3.14). This was the founding of Christ's

---

[1] 'Fellowship is a fruit and not a root' (P. T. Forsyth).

142

koinōnia—or, to use the Hebrew word for a religious associa-
tion of friends, his *Chaburah;* and it was he, not they, who
initiated it (John 15.16).

We need not rehearse the story of the Ministry. Let us
pass to an April evening in the year A.D. 30. It is an Upper
Room in Jerusalem, and, to all human seeming, the *koinōnia*
begun in Galilee, is coming to a sudden and sorrowful end.
But the Host at the table does not think so. Deliberately
he provides for their future fellowship. The simplest, everyday things—bread and wine—he makes 'the love-tokens' of
a fellowship that will continue by and through his death.
After his triumph over death the fellowship will go on, will
grow, will expand.

As it does. Turn to Acts 2.42: 'And they continued
steadfastly . . . in the *koinōnia*.' Though the risen Lord has
returned to his Father, the disciples are not conscious of
being 'orphans' (John 14.18). Had not Jesus promised, 'Lo,
I am with you always', and had not his words come true?
He was still with them, unseen but not unknown, through the
Holy Spirit. They begin to realise that their *koinōnia* is
meant not for themselves alone but for all men, that it is
a fellowship not 'thirled' to the dear, dead days in Galilee
but belonging to the timeless and eternal. It is a fellowship
that even death cannot sever; and when they 'fall asleep'
they know that, having been partners 'in Christ' on earth,
they are but going to be 'with Christ' in his Father's house
with its many rooms (John 14.2).

Nor is it only a continuing fellowship; it is a transforming
one. Gradually, they find that, as they keep the *koinōnia*,
they are becoming different men, so that even their enemies
are constrained to take note that 'these men have been with
Jesus' (Acts 4.13) and are following in his Way'.

III

But this 'vertical' fellowship has its horizontal side also:
'we have fellowship one with another' (1 John 1.7). Right
from the beginning they realised this. 'All that believed,'
we read (Acts 2.44), 'were together.' As every reader of

143

Paul's letters knows, they are full of this Christian 'together-ness'—witness Paul's compound nouns—'fellow-workers', 'fellow-servants', 'fellow-soldiers', 'fellow-heirs'. Call this camaraderie, if you will; but it is a holy camaraderie, a camaraderie 'in Christ', a fellowship in all the burdens and blessings of the Gospel.

But the range of their *koinōnia* goes yet further. 'Our commonwealth,' Paul says, 'is in heaven' (Phil. 3.20); and 'We are compassed about by a great cloud of witnesses,' says the Writer to the Hebrews (12.1). The *koinōnia* in fact stretches 'within the veil'. It embraces both 'the saints on earth' and 'those whose work is done'. It binds together the Church Militant and the Church Triumphant. And its marching song is that of Charles Wesley:

> One family we dwell in him,
> One Church, above, beneath.

60. Diotrephes

(3 John 9)

When Professor Alexander Souter coined the adjective 'diotrephic' to describe an overly ambitious ecclesiastic, his inspiration obviously came from 3 John 9, 'Diotrephes who loveth to have the pre-eminence', or, more simply, 'who likes to be first'.

Originally an epithet 'cherished by Zeus' applied by Homer to kings, Diotrephes in Christ's time had become a proper name. The New Testament bearer of it, who belonged to a local church in the 'diocese' of Ephesus, was manifestly a very forceful personality. Rejecting all apostolic interference in local affairs, he had refused to receive itinerant mission-aries sent by St. John and had even 'expelled' local church-men who wanted to welcome them.

Was he presbyter or incipient bishop? Canon Streeter held

that you cannot be a 'Jack in office' unless the office is already there and went on to suggest that Diotrephes was in fact the first 'monarchical bishop' in Asia. Our doubt is whether there were such 'bishops' as early as this. Is it not just as likely that he was a presbyter—a presbyter with 'a grand memory for forgetting' that he was only such *inter pares?*

Whatever be the truth about Diotrephes, what is the use of having a name which means 'cherished by Zeus' if your conduct is condemned by Christ? 'Whoever wants to be first,' he said, 'must become the willing servant of all' (Mark 10.44).

61. 'Keep yourselves in the love of God'

(Jude 21)

Tucked away near the end of the New Testament and generally ignored by the average Bible reader is a lowly little letter of twenty-five verses written by one Jude. Who (to borrow Thomas Hardy's words) was 'Jude the obscure'? His own answer is 'Servant of Jesus Christ and brother of James'. If, as seems very likely, James is 'the Lord's brother' (Gal. 1.19), Jude is not so obscure after all. He has a yet more distinguished brother. As the Jude of Mark 6.3, he is 'Founder's kin', of the same flesh and blood as the Church's Head.

In his letter, perhaps addressed to a Syrian church and written in defence of 'the faith once for all entrusted to God's people' (Jude 3), Jude attacks some Christian libertines who by their unbelief, irreverence and immorality were disgracing the fair name they bore. It is no part of a Christian's duty to call by soft names those who deserve hard ones— 'dogs must be called dogs and swine swine' observed the old German commentator Bengel when commenting on 'Judge not, that ye be not judged' (Matt. 7.1). So Jude roundly denounces the libertines and warns them of the fearful fate in store for

K 145

them, if they do not mend their ways. But when the vials of his wrath are empty, he turns to address his readers in four noble imperatives (Jude 20f.).

It is for the third of these, if for nothing else, that Jude serves a claim on our remembrance. 'Keep yourselves in the love of God' says Jude—that is, if we may paraphrase his words and bring out their meaning, 'Stay on in the shelter of God's love for you'. As 'single-speech' Hamilton is remembered for one solitary and celebrated utterance in the House of Commons, so Jude the obscure deserves to be remembered for the six words of his third imperative.

'Keep yourselves in the love of God.' But are not the faithful, according to St. Peter, 'kept by the power of God' till full salvation comes (1 Peter 1.5)? Yes, God keeps the faithful. Nonetheless, since God has given men free will, it is always possible for some to sin themselves out of the shelter of the divine love. God's grace is the *prius*—the prior thing— in our salvation; but for its outcome God is dependent on man as man is on God. His loving vigilance must be matched by man's vigilant effort—what we call Christian perseverance.

How then do we keep ourselves in the love of God? By maintaining the 'I-thou' relationship between ourselves and God which we call prayer. By reading the Bible which is (in Robertson Smith's phrase) 'the only record of the redeeming love of God'. By worship in the company of God's faithful people, for (as the plain man told John Wesley on a historic occasion) 'the Bible knows nothing of solitary religion'. By serving our fellow-men in love, for to love one's brother, according to St. John, is proof that we know God—or, rather, are known by him (1 John 3.14, 4.20).

Yet our ultimate security rests not on our own efforts but on the power of a 'keeping' God; and to this, in his very last—and magnificent—words Jude returns:

'Glory be to him who can keep you from falling and bring you safe to his glorious presence, innocent and happy. To God, the only God, who saves us through Jesus Christ our Lord, be the glory, majesty, authority and power which he had before time began, now and for ever.' (Jerusalem Bible).

146

It is Jude's way of saying, 'Look unto him and be saved'. My friend Donald Smith, author of *And All the Trumpets,* tells how, during World War II, the Japanese suddenly confronted by a brawling Malayan river, made their British prisoners rig up a slender bridge from bamboo stems, and then invited them to scramble across it,—or be pushed into the river. One or two did manage to negotiate the swaying bamboos successfully. But when Donald's own turn came, he looked down into the torrent and stood stock-still in terror. The guard stood ready with rifle and bayonet to prod him into action when, from the other side, a friend's voice said quietly, 'Don't look down, just keep your eyes fixed on my face.' He did so, and was safe.

That 'earthly story' surely has a 'heavenly meaning'.

62. The Revelation of Jesus Christ

(Revelation 1.1.)

'Revelation in Greek is *apokalypsis* which means 'unveiling' and gives us our word 'apocalypse'. In the last book of the New Testament it signifies that 'unveiling' of God's future in Christ that came, by inspiration of the Spirit, to a Christian seer and prophet called John, whom the Romans had imprisoned for his faith on the rocky isle of Patmos off the coast of Asia Minor (modern Turkey).

Many of us seem to have an 'apocalyptic' streak in our make-up. We see it in the little lass who, on being told that 'granny had gone to be with God', was heard to comment, 'Gosh, how posh!' (Somehow she divined that, though it had been 'sad' for Granny, it was going to be all right now that she had gone to be with 'the Good Man above'.) So those of us who believe in God as the Lord of history are fain, in time of tragedy or disaster, to 'lift the veil' to look beyond history's lowering horizons, and to glimpse what good things God has prepared for those who love him.

Likewise in the last decades of the first century A.D., when the might of imperial Rome was turned menacingly on the little Church of Christ, and many Christians were being martyred because they refused to join in the official worship of the Roman emperor, it was natural that a Christian leader like John should seek to comfort and encourage his fellow-Christians in Asia Minor by 'unveiling' the future God had in store for them as well as for pagan Rome and its persecuting emperors like Nero and Domitian. John's 'apocalypse' took the form of a series of visions, with a prologue and an epilogue; glorious visions of God and his Christ, horrendous visions of the impending judgments on the enemies of God's people, and blessed visions of the final felicity of the faithful in the eternal City of God.

For many centuries John's book was like a cryptogram to which the code had been lost, and some Christians like Martin Luther even doubted whether it was a truly Christian book and should stand in the New Testament. Now, thanks to the labours of scholars like R. H. Charles over the last hundred years, we understand better the true nature of apocalyptic writing, and the meaning of 'the least read and most mis-understood book of the New Testament' can be made reason-ably clear to all who are prepared to go through it with a good commentary.

What is the first point we must seize if we are to under-stand this book which has so long been a happy hunting-ground for crackpots? It is that John's visions of the judg-ment and victory of God were originally very much 'a tract for the times' written to strengthen the resolution of the Church on earth in a time of bitter persecution, by prophesy-ing the downfall of Rome the persecutor. Most of the imagery for his tract John draws from the Old Testament (particularly the book of Daniel which is a Jewish apocalypse). This enables him to refer to the enemy Rome under the guise of the old enemy Babylon (Cf. Rev. 18.2 'Fallen, fallen is Babylon the great!') and so, while making his meaning plain to his readers, to conceal it by his cipher-language from hostile eyes.

Does this mean that, because John's book was directed

to a particular historical situation near the end of the first century, it has no Word of God for us in the twentieth? On the contrary, those who 'have ears to hear' what John is saying will find that, if they wrestle with his visions, he has much that is Christian to say to us who live in times hardly less troubled and 'apocalyptic' than his own. John is not peddling second-hand Jewish apocalyptic ideas with a Christian veneer. He is telling us that this world of ours, with all that is good in it as God's handiwork, with all its evil as the result of men's sins and follies, is the arena of God's redeeming purpose. The Cross of Christ is the key and clue to the mystery which encompasses us, and the challenge is thrown down to God's people in every age to stand firm in their faith, even unto death, in the confidence that God's great purposes will be fulfilled.

James Denney once compared Revelation to a tunnel with light at the beginning and light at the end and, in the middle, 'a long stretch of darkness through which lurid objects thunder past, bewildering and stunning the reader'. This is another way of saying that the great central section of the book (chapters 6-16) which contains a series of mounting judgments—seven seals, seven trumpets, seven bowls—forms by far the toughest part of it for the ordinary student. Therefore if he is appalled by the prospect of 'lurid objects thundering past' him, let the reader accept the advice of an old Scots worthy and 'just take a trot up and down the seven kirks of Asia' (chapters 1-3) and then turn to the closing chapters (21-22) which depict the eternal City of God. More than anything else in the New Testament these chapters have served to make heaven real for many Christians and nerved them to do battle with the world and its evils, 'knowing that their labour is not in vain in the Lord'.

But, take it all in all, the dominant feature of the last book of the Bible is its ultimate optimism. Reinhold Niebuhr once wrote a book with the title *Beyond Tragedy*. It is John the Seer's 'beyond tragedy' optimism—the optimism that has looked into the very abyss of earthly evil and is yet unaffrighted because it knows that the world belongs to God and not to the devil—which is his finest Word of God to us.

John knows that 'the evil world cannot win at last because it failed to win the only time it ever could. It is a vanquished world in which men play their devilries. Christ has overcome it'. The words are P. T. Forsyth's, but they express John's meaning.

63. Apocalyptic Numbers

(Revelation 13.18)

'I have often admired the mystical way of Pythagoras', confessed Sir Thomas Browne, 'and the secret magic of numbers'. He has not been alone. Whether Greek philosophers or Jewish cabbalists, men have long been fascinated by numbers, finding in them symbolical or secret significances. Even in these 'Space days' numbers have not lost their mystical attraction for popular thinking. 'Third time's lucky' we say, hoping it may be so, though we would probably be stumped to give a reason why. Sailors who refuse to put to sea on the 13th of the month, Italians who never use the number 13 in their lotteries, Parisians who avoid it for their houses, all testify to the 'unluckiness' of 13. It is a belief—or rather, superstition—that goes back, we are told, to a banquet in the Scandinavian Valhalla when, with 13 present, Balder son of Odin was slain, but which was certainly confirmed for Christians by the number of persons in the Upper Room.

But there is a good deal more to this business of numbers. Those versed in the ancient languages know that the Greeks and the Hebrews used the letters of their alphabets as numerals; and inevitably this double function of the alphabet tempted the ingenious to turn a number into a name—or a name into a number. For an instance: some years before the city was overwhelmed by Vesuvius in 79 A.D., a young man scribbled on a wall in Pompeii, 'I love her whose number is *phi mu epsilon*'—three letters of the Greek alphabet which add up to 545.

The Hebrews however had a way of treating numbers as theological symbols. Sacred for them were such numbers as three, four, seven and twelve, as a glance at the article 'numbers' in any Bible dictionary will show. And when you try to unravel the mysteries of the last book of the Bible, you discover how important it is to have a rough key to the Seer's mystical arithmetic. If 3—in (3.12) there are three names; in (4.8) there are three 'Holies'—may be called the number of heaven, 4—the number of the winds or the corners of the world—is that of earth. Add 3 and 4 together and you get the perfect number 7—the number of the seals in God's book of destiny (5.1) as well as of many other things in Revelation. On the other hand, when we read of 'a time and times, and half a time' (12.14) i.e. $3\frac{1}{2}$ years, this 'broken' 7 has a sinister ring and signifies a time of persecution for God's people. 12—the number of the tribes of Israel, of Christ's apostles and of the gates of the heavenly City (21.12)—may be called the 'church' number; so, when Rev. 7.4 mentions its multiple 144,000—12 times 12 multiplied by 1000—John means us to think of the vast completeness of the Church Triumphant.

But the apocalyptic number *par excellence* is undoubtedly 666. We once asked a noted New Testament scholar the number of his house in Oxford. 'Half the number of the Beast', he replied. He was referring to Rev. 13.18. In that chapter John tells of the appearance on earth of a truly diabolical 'beast' who is permitted to make war on the people of God and to slay all those who will not worship his bestial majesty. If John had set down this beast's real name, what trouble he might have saved readers of the Bible down succeeding centuries! But to have done so would of course have been highly dangerous, both for himself and his readers. Instead he gave his readers a numerical clue which he hoped would suffice:

'Here is the key, and anyone who has intelligence may work out the number of the beast. The number represents a man's name; and the numerical value of its letters is six hundred and sixty-six.' (NEB.)

666—each of the digits, observe, falling short of the perfect

151

number 7. What sinister suggestion is here? Who is the man the letters of whose name add up to 666?

When the Seer gave his readers the clue—one which they surely followed—he not only gave the cabbalistically-minded their finest opportunity, but, all unwittingly, he encouraged many persecuted saints, down the centuries, to find the beast in the tyrants of their own day.

In the fourth century some found the prophecy come true in Julian the Apostate who stripped the Church of most of its privileges. A few centuries later, Christians were discovering him in Mahomet. After the Reformation Protestants identified the beast with the Pope of Rome, whereupon Catholics retorted by casting Luther for the role. So, last century, when Napoleon was bestriding Europe like a terrible colossus, or, even in our own time, when Hitler was menacing the free world with his devilries, there were men to say, 'Here is the beast foreseen by John of Patmos'.

That they were all mistaken needs no saying. The beast of Revelation belongs to the first century. That he represents pagan Rome—Rome the persecutor of the Church of Christ in the last decades of the first century—is certain. But who in particular? Well, take the Greek words NERON KESAR, turn them into Hebrew (which has no vowels), add up the numerical value of the Hebrew consonants, and you get 666. In short, the likeliest candidate for the bestial honour is the mad, bad Emperor Nero who instigated the first great persecution of the Church and who (rumour had it later) was about to return from the dead and continue his 'beastliness' (Cf. Rev. 13.3 which almost certainly refers to this.)

What does our discussion show? This at least that modern Biblical criticism has its value—even if it is only the negative one of delivering us from the aberrations of misguided mortals who would turn the book of Revelation into a precise and divinely-inspired 'pre-view' of the whole future course of history.

64. The Holy City

(Revelation 21.2)

There are some people who when they get a new book cannot resist the temptation to read the last chapter first, to see how it all will end. Nor are they greatly to be blamed if their book is Revelation. In its long middle stretches, to mystify and even repel, there is 'the devil's own plenty' of darkness and doom, of plagues and conflagrations and catastrophes, of dragons and beasts and monsters of the Pit, till all reaches a climax in the final battle between the armies of heaven and the legions of hell, and the Last Judgment. But when at length we grope our way to the end of the 'tunnel', suddenly, with chapter 21, the world of the past is gone, and there breaks upon our view the splendour of a new creation. Rapt by the Spirit to a high mountain-top, the Seer sees 'the holy city, the new Jerusalem, coming down from God out of heaven, as beautiful as a bride dressed for her husband'. It shone, he tells us, with 'all the radiant glory of God'. Twelve gates it had, each of them a pearl with the name of one of the tribes of Israel on it; its wall, which towered 1500 miles high, had written on its foundation stones the names of the twelve apostles; and the city itself, a marvel of pure gold, had the shape of a cube (for the ancients, the pattern of perfection). Through the streets of the City flowed the river of the water of life, with, on either bank, the tree of life whose leaves were for the healing of the nations. The vision culminates in a glimpse of God and the Lamb enthroned, the worship of the Church Triumphant, and the sound of a Hallelujah Chorus.

Yet this grand finale is not altogether unprepared for. All through the preceding visions of judgment, from the opening of the sealed book in chapter 5, the Seer, by means of his wonderful 'parentheses' or 'interludes'—the vision of the redeemed martyrs in heaven, the triumph song of Moses and the Lamb, the nuptials of the Lamb and his Bride (which is the Church)—has been giving us seraphic fore-glimpses of the high glories of heaven. At last, in chapter 21, like a new Moses, John stands on Pisgah and surveys for us the Promised Land, 'the home of God's elect'.

What are we Christians nowadays to make of this Pisgah view from Patmos?

Time was when our literalising forefathers regarded this part of Revelation as a divinely-inspired ordnance map of Paradise. Many a heavenly geography has been set down on paper, many a chart made of the new Jerusalem, many a classified directory compiled of its citizens. If we no longer go in for this celestial geographising, it is because we now know better how to interpret the Seer's trance-like visions and mystic numbers. His interest lies in symbols rather than statistics; his true point is the ineffable magnitude and perfection of the Eternal City. This is why he almost bursts the bonds of language to describe the indescribable and suggest:

> Glory beyond all glory ever seen
> By waking sense or by the dreaming soul.

In fact the Seer's priceless legacy to Christendom has not been his apocalyptic architectonics but his profound and evocative images. It is not the celestial map-makers but the Christian poets who have best caught his meaning and used his 'Pisgah view' to instruct Christian piety and kindle Christian hope, whether it be Bernard of Morlaix's 'Jerusalem the Golden', the anonymous Song of Mary 'Hierusalem, my happy home' or even—though it falls far short of these two—the strains of 'The Holy City' beloved by so many Victorians.

Can they still do this for us today, when men are much more interested in the 'secular' city than the 'holy' one, and when a modern Christian prophet has wisely warned us that we should not 'claim any knowledge of either the furniture of heaven or the temperature of hell'? Must we indeed mournfully dismiss John's vision as but the fantasy of an over-wrought Oriental imagination utterly incredible to Christians in a scientific age?

154

In answer two things may be said, one general and the other particular.

To begin with, all our Christian ideas about the Last Things are basically transpositions into the key of the Hereafter of that revelation of God which we already have 'in the face of Jesus Christ'. (Our clue, for example, to the Second Coming must be the first coming.) In other words, we apply to the life beyond death the great argument of St. Paul, 'He who did not spare his own son but gave him up for us all, will he not also give us all things with him. . . . For I am persuaded that neither death nor life . . . will be able to separate us from the love of God in Christ Jesus our Lord' (Rom. 8.32,38f). The Christian faith in a blessed life hereafter is an inference from the doctrine of our redemption. The God who cared, and cares for us, will care for us for ever—care for us till past all darkness, danger and death, we shall see him 'face to face'.

Second, for John the Seer his visions of heaven were the fruit not of his own untutored imagination but of the revealing Spirit of God. 'I was in the Spirit on the Lord's Day' he tells us at the beginning (1.10), and at the end (21.10) 'In the Spirit he carried me away to a great high mountain'. Now if we hold that it is the Spirit's role to 'take of the things of Christ and show them' to his followers and to 'declare what is to come' (John 16.13f), it follows that the Seer's pictures of 'Jerusalem the Golden' were inspired by the Spirit of God. To be sure, they take the form of highly-coloured apocalyptic visions—what many would call 'myths'. 'Myths' they may be, but, as the poet says,

> Myth is the language that contains the clue
> To that which is at once both real and true.[1]

Provided we remember that John's visions are not charts of heaven, but inspired instructions to faith, they may still speak to us of the true nature of that 'hope which is laid up for us in heaven'.

What have they to tell us?

First, at the end of the Christian road is a city—the City

[1] R. W. Stewart.

155

of God. In other words, the consummation of the Christian hope is supremely social. It is no 'flight of the alone to the Alone' but life in the redeemed community of heaven. More, heaven means belonging for ever to the family of God, 'I will be his God, and he shall be my son' (Rev. 21.7).

Next, whatever else heaven means, it means an end to all the evils and sorrows of earth. 'God,' says the heavenly voice, 'will wipe away every tear from their eyes, and death shall be no more, neither shall there be mourning or crying nor pain any more, for the former things have passed away' (Rev. 21.4).

Finally, heaven must mean the Beatific Vision. When John says 'They shall see his face' (Rev. 22.4) he echoes his Lord's beatitude, 'Blessed are the pure in heart, for they shall see God' (Matt. 5.8):

> The King there in his beauty
> Without a veil is seen.

To behold the God before whom angels veil their faces, the God who created us and, in Christ, redeemed us, who so loved his lost and wandering children that he came right down among us to show us what he is like and then died on a Cross to save us from our sins and make us heirs of life eternal, and, beholding him, to behold all things in him and in the light of his redemption, this truly

> were a well spent journey
> Though seven deaths lay between.

And, if they serve to purify our spirits for this inconceivable reward of God's grace, the sorrows and sufferings of earth will not seem altogether meaningless or vain. To see God and his Christ—the Lamb that once was slain—face to face amid the fellowship and worship of the Church Triumphant, this surely is the end of all ends, the final solution to the riddle of life, the consummation of all love and desire.

Hon on Thou 39

Cup 42

2 Cor 11 19 'Who is offended, & I burn not'

1 Thess 5 19-22 12 3ff

NT 'hymns'. 117, 128

'Flesh' qua theology / 129

Parishioner = pilgrim 137

Lexicon → presence of Θ 141

'Revs' of tunnel 149